I0804939

Martin Luther
~ *on* ~
Holy Baptism

Martin Luther ~ *on* ~ Holy Baptism

Sermons to the People (1525–39)

EDITED BY

Benjamin T. G. Mayes

CONCORDIA PUBLISHING HOUSE · SAINT LOUIS

3558 S. Jefferson Ave., St. Louis, MO 63118-3968
1-800-325-3040 • www.cph.org

Unless otherwise indicated, Scripture quotations in this volume are translated from Luther's writings or from Luther's German Bible.

Quotations marked AE are from *Luther's Works*, American Edition: volumes 1–30 © 1955–76 and volumes 57–60, 67–69, 75–79 © 2009–16 Concordia Publishing House; volumes 31–54 © 1957–86 Augsburg Fortress.

Manufactured in the United States of America

Library of Congress Cataloging-in-Publication Data

Names: Luther, Martin, 1483–1546, author. | Mayes, Benjamin T. G., editor.

Title: Martin Luther on holy Baptism : sermons to the people 1525–39 / edited by Benjamin T. G. Mayes.

Description: Saint Louis : Concordia Publishing House, 2018. | Includes bibliographical references and index.

Identifiers: LCCN 2018013754 (print) | LCCN 2018021485 (ebook) | ISBN 9780758659736 | ISBN 9780758659729 (alk. paper)

Subjects: LCSH: Baptism—Sermons. | Baptism—History of doctrines—16th century.

Classification: LCC BR333.5.B3 (ebook) | LCC BR333.5.B3 L8813 2018 (print) | DDC 234/.161—dc23

LC record available at https://lccn.loc.gov/201801375

---

4 5 6 7 8 9 10 11 28 27 26 25

CONTENTS

To the Christian Reader vii

Introduction xiii

Martin Luther on Holy Baptism

1. Infant Baptism and Faith That Is Not One's Own (1525) 3
2. Sermons on Holy Baptism (1534) 13
3. Sermons on Holy Baptism (1538) 61
4. Sermons on Holy Baptism (1539) 101

Study Questions 119

Abbreviations 123

Index of Persons and Groups 125

Scripture Index 127

TO THE CHRISTIAN READER

Grace and peace in Christ the Lord!

Of all the events in the life of Jesus Christ, the ones mentioned by all four evangelists must surely not be considered unimportant. Just as the death and resurrection of Jesus is at the heart of the New Testament's message, so is Baptism. The Baptism of Jesus marked the beginning of His ministry in each of the Gospels and was a miraculous event in which the three persons of the Trinity were made known (Matt. 3:13–17; Mark 1:9–11; Luke 3:21–22; John 1:32–34).

Baptism is the foundational sacrament of Christianity. It is the Christian's primary encounter with God in His mercy. According to the baptismal command of the Lord Jesus, Baptism, along with teaching, is how a person becomes His disciple (Matt. 28:19). No one can enter the kingdom of God unless he is born again of water and the Spirit (John 3:1–5). Baptism according to the New Testament is powerful unto salvation. Baptism saves us (1 Pet. 3:21; Titus 3:3–8). It sprinkles our hearts clean from an evil conscience (Heb. 10:23; Eph. 5:26; 1 Cor. 6:11). It clothes us with Christ (Gal. 3:26–28; 1 Cor. 12:13). And it gives us participation in the death and resurrection of Christ (Col. 2:11, 20; 3:1, 3–4; Rom. 6:4). Thus, according to the New Testament, Baptism is important for salvation and is not a mere ceremony.

And yet the saving power of holy Baptism is often attacked, even by sincere Christians. One example of this is Wayne Grudem in his *Systematic Theology.*[1] Grudem sees Baptim only as *man's* act of obedience and confession, not as God's action toward the human being. As a result, he sees it as untruthful to give Baptism to infants, since infants cannot confess faith. His unproved assumption is that infants cannot believe, and therefore whenever the New Testament connects Baptism with faith, he sees infants as being excluded from Baptism. This approach denies that Baptism, analogous to the Word of the Gospel, is the power of God unto salvation, and it also assumes, but does not prove, that infants cannot believe.

[1] Wayne Grudem, *Systematic Theology: An Introduction to Biblical Doctrine* (Grand Rapids: Zondervan, 1994), pp. 966–87.

Another challenge comes from Presbyterian pastor Patrick Ramsey, who argues not about what the New Testament says, but simply tries to prove that Martin Luther's doctrine of baptismal power and regeneration conflicts with his doctrine of justification by faith alone.[2] A simple answer is that Scripture teaches both baptismal regeneration and justification by faith alone, so the matter is settled, whether or not the two truths seem to conflict with each other. But a more careful reading of Luther shows that Baptism and justification by faith alone do not at all conflict. Similar to the Word of the Gospel, Baptism is God's work which man simply receives. And the benefits that God promises in holy Baptism must be received through faith. Because Ramsey sees Baptism as the work of man instead of the work of God which man simply receives, similar to hearing the preaching of the Gospel, he cannot but see Luther's doctrine of baptismal regeneration as incompatible with justification *sola fide*.[3]

To these examples others could be added. They show that the topic of Baptism can lead to heated disagreements. Yet because of the praises that the New Testament gives to Baptism, including the miraculous Trinitarian theophany at the Baptism of Christ, which was to fulfill all righteousness (Matt. 3:15), it is important that Baptism be learned, studied, preached, heard, and treasured as the Christian's precious jewel.[4]

Not Just a One-Time Benefit

At Luther's time, a group called the "Anabaptists" based Baptism's validity on human faith. In their view, which is similar to modern Baptist views regarding this sacrament, Baptism is an act symbolizing rebirth, a kind of confession that Christians make to show that they truly believe. For them, Baptism has no saving power. But this was not the only error that Luther confronted. The other error was one he found underlying the Roman Catholic sacramental system. Namely, he had been raised to regard Baptism as being very limited in its benefits. Although it purified a person from previous sins, if

[2] D. Patrick Ramsey, "Sola Fide Compromised? Martin Luther and the Doctrine of Baptism," *Themelios* 34, no. 2 (2009): 179–93.

[3] Ramsey ("Sola Fide Compromised?" p. 191) also accuses Luther of sacerdotalism: Baptism is necessary for salvation, but Baptism may only be given by pastors (he says); therefore, the salvation of people depends on pastors. But Ramsey fails to see that Luther allows and encourages emergency lay Baptism (see below, pp. 116–17). This fact undermines Ramsey's minor premise. Thus, for Luther, salvation does not depend on pastors, even though they are the ordinary ministers of Baptism outside of cases of emergency.

[4] "We have, therefore, no greater jewel in body and soul, for by it we are made holy and are saved, which no other kind of life, no work upon earth, can attain" (Luther, *Large Catechism* [152]) IV 26, in W. H. T. Dau and F. Bente, eds., *Triglot Concordia: The Symbolical Books of the Ev. Lutheran Church, German-Latin-English* [St. Louis: Concordia 1921], p. 743).

one was baptized as an infant (as most people of that time in Europe were) and if infants have no actual sins (as some people think), then Baptism would remove only original sin. That is to say, practically speaking, for most people Baptism was seen as having no saving benefit. It was a prerequisite for salvation, to be sure, but what would save a person would have to be something else, since Baptism applied only to past sins.

Luther's solution, based on the teaching of Scripture, was to elevate the significance of Baptism over what he found taught by the early church fathers. Over and over again Luther criticizes a statement he found in several letters of Jerome: that Baptism is like a ship on the open seas; that by post-baptismal sin the ship is wrecked; and that in this situation penitence is the "second plank" to which a Christian must cling if he wants to be saved.[5] That is, as Luther had read and heard Jerome's statement in the Roman Catholic Church, Baptism completely freed a person of sin, but if afterward one were to sin, the effect of Baptism is gone. In this case, the sacrament of penance must be sought. If Baptism is a ship, then post-baptismal sin causes a shipwreck, and all you can do is hold onto some of the wreckage, a "second plank."[6]

Against this, Luther taught that Baptism brings not just initial benefits but also ongoing benefits. This emphasis on the ongoing benefits of Baptism was new at the Reformation. The Roman Church previously had taught only the initial benefits of Baptism: total purification from all sins, original and actual. But what about after that? When someone sins after Baptism (whether the sin is serious or not), does Baptism help him anymore? According to the theology of the Roman Catholic Church, it does not. Luther explained: "For no sooner had we taken off the children's shoes, and they had emerged from the blessed font, then they [the Papists] took it all away by this preaching: 'You lost Baptism and soiled your christening gown long ago by sinning; so now you have to think about repenting of your sin and making satisfaction for it by fasting, praying, going on pilgrimages, and making endowments until you are reconciled to God and so return to His favor.' "[7]

If penitence is taken in the sense of the sacrament of penance, with its requirement of the satisfaction of works as a requisite for forgiveness, and

[5] See Jerome, Ep. 130.9 to Demetrius (NPNF[2] 6:266); Ep 122.4 to Rusticus (NPNF[2] 6:229); and Ep. 147.3 to Sabianus (NPNF[2] 6:291). I have not found Jerome saying that Baptism is the ship that is wrecked by sins, though he certainly speaks of certain post-baptismal sins as causing "shipwreck," possibly an allusion to 1 Tim. 1:19, and in these cases one can be saved by clinging to the "plank" of penitence. But he thinks not all people need to do this. Many people, he says, have not suffered shipwreck.

[6] See *Large Catechism* (1529) IV 80–82 (Kolb-Wengert, p. 466; *Concordia*, pp. 430–31). See also Luther, *Babylonian Captivity of the Church* (1520), AE 36:58.

[7] Below, pp. 47–48; cf. below, pp. 50–51.

if monastic vows are seen as equal to Baptism, and if Baptism removes only previous sins, then the actual significance of Baptism for Christian salvation can only be as a prerequisite for salvation, but not actually saving. The saving, in this scheme, has been shifted to humanly devised works. Instead of this, Luther emphasizes that Baptism is an unsinkable ship. Intentional, persistent post-baptismal sin does not destroy the ship of Baptism, but rather causes you to fall overboard. Repentance, in Luther's view, is how you hold on to the ship until you can climb back onboard.[8] Through repentance the saving benefits of Baptism are ever available to us. Through repentance we partake once again of the saving power of Baptism.[9] "Even if I fall from it, I am nevertheless baptized and am a Christian. I am baptized in God's water, not by some washing maid, not by Gabriel or by the pastor or bishop or pope, but by God the Father, Son, and Holy Spirit."[10]

Luther as a Guide

Martin Luther is a good guide to Baptism. Several times during his ministry he preached sermon series on Baptism to the people of Wittenberg, and in recent years some of these sermons have been translated into English. The present volume brings together three of those sermons series from the 1530s, plus a selection on infant Baptism from 1525. In these sermons Luther teaches about

- The connection between Baptism and faith
- What faith is
- The role of pastors as ministers of Baptism
- The meaning of the words "In the name of the Father and of the Son and of the Holy Spirit"
- The distinction between Baptism's validity regardless of faith and its benefit, which is received through faith alone
- The Baptism of Christ
- Atonement
- The ongoing benefits of Baptism in the life of a Christian
- What "salvation" means
- Sacraments as signs of God's saving will toward us
- God's will and revelation

---

[8] *Large Catechism* (1529) IV 80–82 (Kolb-Wengert, p. 466; *Concordia*, pp. 430–31).

[9] See below, pp. 54–55.

[10] Below, pp. 111–12.

- Baptismal liturgy and ceremonies
- Baptism as covenant
- Repentance as a return to Baptism
- The importance of God's commands for certainty of faith and conscience
- Infant Baptism and infant faith
- Emergency Baptism by laypeople

With his profound scriptural insight and depth of pastoral wisdom, Luther is a good guide to Baptism, especially in his sermons to the people.

This Book

This book was imagined as a result of two events. First, as I have worked on editing translations of Luther's sermons for the past decade, I discovered these sermon series on Baptism by accident, by reading through lists of the reformer's sermons.[11] Second, while teaching at Concordia Theological Seminary (Fort Wayne, Indiana) in our *Theologia* course on Baptism, I desired a book that would bring together some of Luther's best sermons on Baptism, for use as a course text and for Christians to read and discuss. Luther wrote several books on the Lord's Supper, but no full-length books on Baptism. By putting his Baptism sermon series together, we would finally have a full book by Luther on holy Baptism.

Each chapter of the present book may be read by individuals or by groups. Study questions at the end of the book promote deeper thinking on the topics that Luther discusses. Each question gives page numbers to the sermons where the answers (or more food for thought) may be found. Scholars, too, may find the book of interest, since it presents rich material from Luther on Baptism that has been overlooked in nearly all previous examinations of Luther's theology, even specialized studies on Luther's doctrine of Baptism.[12]

This book is the work of several people. The translator of most of the volume was Mr. Matthew Carver; some parts were translated by the Rev. James L. Langebartels and by Dr. Christopher Boyd Brown. Dawn Mirly

[11] In Kurt Aland, *Hilfsbuch Zum Lutherstudium*, 4th ed. (Bielefeld: Luther-Verlag, 1996).

[12] The exception is Robert Kolb, "'What Benefit Does the Soul Receive from a Handful of Water?': Luther's Preaching on Baptism, 1528–1539," *Concordia Journal* 25, no. 4 (1999): 346–63. Isolated passages of these sermons are mentioned also by Ulrich Asendorf, *Die Theologie Martin Luthers nach seinen Predigten* (Göttingen: Vandenhoeck & Ruprecht, 1988), pp. 288, 293. Lorenz Grönvik, *Die Taufe in der Theologie Martin Luthers* (Âbo: Âbo Akademi, 1968), makes use of the 1534 Baptism sermons.

Weinstock, my longtime colleague with the Luther's Works project at Concordia Publishing House, was the copyeditor for this book. The entire team at Concordia Publishing House brought the book into the light of day and is responsible for putting it into the reader's hands.

May these sermons bless you, Christian reader, and lead you to hold to and believe more firmly in the gracious baptismal promises of the Father, Son, and Holy Spirit, the most blessed and all-holy Trinity.

Benjamin T. G. Mayes
The Epiphany of Our Lord
January 6, 2018 A+D

INTRODUCTION

Luther's Sermons on Baptism

If one thinks of how much Martin Luther wrote about the Lord's Supper and about preaching and compares that with what he published about Baptism, it might be tempting to think that Baptism was not very important to him. Luther wrote lengthy treatises against Ulrich Zwingli on the Lord's Supper, but there are no such treatises on Baptism. Instead of treatises, most of Luther's focused, intentional writing on Baptism occurred in sermons or in his catechisms. Why did he not write treatises on Baptism? Perhaps it was because the challenge to the Sacrament of Baptism came not from scholars or church leaders, but from wandering Anabaptist preachers who were often uneducated lay preachers. Since Luther did not have an official representative of Anabaptist theology to debate, and since his hearers, nevertheless, had to be warned to avoid those preachers, he put his doctrine of Baptism into writing directed to the laity: catechisms and sermons. As a result, high-level reflection on the doctrine of Baptism might not be found clearly in Luther's works. Nevertheless, Luther's writings are rich in baptismal teaching. Many of his writings and sermons that address Baptism are known and have been translated into English, for example:

- *Holy and Blessed Sacrament of Baptism* (1519), AE 35:23–43
- *Babylonian Captivity of the Church* (1520), "The Sacrament of Baptism," AE 36:57–81
- 1525 *Lent Postil* (part of the *Church Postil*), sermon for Epiphany 3 on Matt. 8:1–13, "Infant Baptism and Faith That Is Not One's Own," AE 76:257–66
- *Concerning Rebaptism* (1528), AE 40:225–62
- *Ten Sermons on the Catechism* (1528), "Sermon on Baptism," AE 51:182–88
- *Small Catechism* and *Large Catechism* (1529), "The Sacrament of Holy Baptism"
- Sermon on John 1:29–34 (November 3, 1537), AE 22:158–81

- *Sermons at the Baptism of Bernhard of Anhalt* (April 1–2, 1540), AE 58:33–49; 51:313–29
- Sermon on Matt. 3:13–17 (January 13, 1544), AE 58:71–78
- Sermon on Matt. 3:13–17 (January 6, 1546), AE 58:357–69[1]

These baptismal writings have been thoroughly, if not exhaustively, researched.[2]

These are not the only documents in which Luther taught the Sacrament of Baptism. Luther also preached several sermon series on Baptism.[3] In January and February, from 1528 to 1539, Luther sometimes interrupted the readings of the seasons of Epiphany, pre-Lent, and Lent to focus on this sacrament. Although the 1533 Wittenberg church order did not specifically call for preaching on Baptism during the Epiphany or pre-Lent season,[4] the lectionary printed in Luther's German Bible beginning in 1526, reflecting Wittenberg practice, noted that the Sunday after Epiphany was to be observed as the Festival of Christ's Baptism,[5] anticipating by about 450 years the current practice (in The Lutheran Church—Missouri Synod, at least). At the beginning of his Baptism sermon series, Luther often notes that in ancient times the Feast of Epiphany commemorated three "miracles": the Magi, the wedding at Cana, and Christ's Baptism; and he notes

[1] Jonathan Trigg has shown also that Luther's *Lectures on Genesis* (1535–45), AE 1–8, are rich in baptismal teaching. Jonathan D. Trigg, *Baptism in the Theology of Martin Luther* (Leiden: Brill, 1994).

[2] Charles L. Cortright, "Luther on Infant Baptism: On Rebaptism (1528) and the Large Catechism (1529)," in *Reformation 500: The Enduring Relevance of the Lutheran Reformation*, ed. Curtis A. Jahn (Milwaukee: Northwestern, 2017), pp. 73–92; Bernhard Lohse, *Martin Luther's Theology: Its Historical and Systematic Development*, trans. Roy A. Harrisville (Minneapolis: Fortress, 1999), pp. 299–301; Mark D. Tranvik, "Luther on Baptism," *Lutheran Quarterly* 13, no. 1 (1999): 75–90; David P. Scaer, *Baptism*, Confessional Lutheran Dogmatics 11 (St. Louis: Luther Academy, 1999); David P. Scaer, "Luther, Baptism, and the Church Today," *Concordia Theological Quarterly* 62, no. 4 (1998): 247–68; Byran D. Spinks, "Luther's Timely Theology of Unilateral Baptism," *Lutheran Quarterly* 9, no. 1 (1995): 23–45; Paul H. Zietlow, "Martin Luther's Arguments for Infant Baptism," *Concordia Journal* 20, no. 2 (1994): 147–71; Gerald S. Krispin, "Baptism and *Heilsgewissheit* in Luther's Theology," *Concordia Journal* 13, no. 2 (1987): 106–18; Jaroslav Pelikan, "Luther's Defense of Infant Baptism," in *Luther for an Ecumenical Age*, ed. Carl S. Meyer (St. Louis: Concordia, 1967), pp. 200–218; Paul Althaus, *The Theology of Martin Luther*, trans. Robert C. Schultz (Philadelphia: Fortress, 1966), pp. 353–74; Werner Jetter, *Die Taufe beim jungen Luther* (Tübingen: Mohr, 1954); Julius Köstlin, *The Theology of Luther in Its Historical Development and Inner Harmony*, trans. Charles E. Hay, 2 vols. (Philadelphia: Lutheran Publication Society, 1897), 2:507–11.

[3] For scholarly analysis and use of these sermons, see the sources mentioned above, p. xi n. 12.

[4] Emil Sehling, ed., *Die Evangelischen Kirchenordnungen Des XVI. Jahrhunderts*, vol. 1.1 (Leipzig: O. R. Reisland, 1902), pp. 700–710.

[5] *Register der Episteln und Evangelien* (1526), WA DB 7:533–34.

that the practice of the Wittenberg church was to focus on Baptism in the season of Epiphany. Several times Luther expanded the liturgical celebration of Baptism into the following weeks. He preached these sermon series on Baptism in 1528, 1531, 1532, 1534, 1538, and 1539.

Luther's emphases in his baptismal teaching developed throughout his career. In 1520, in the *Babylonian Captivity of the Church*, Luther's focus was on the Roman Catholic teaching of Baptism, which saw little significance for this sacrament after the first big post-baptismal sin. In the mind-set of the medieval church, Baptism was effective for cleansing a person from previous sins, but not for sins that might follow Baptism. For that, one had to resort to the sacrament of penance. This error regarding Baptism remained one of Luther's battlefronts throughout his life.

The other front was against the Anabaptists. In the 1525 *Lent Postil* (part of the *Church Postil*), Luther's focus was on the Anabaptists, who made an argument like this: Only those who believe should be baptized; infants cannot believe; therefore, they should not be baptized. In the *Lent Postil*, Luther addresses this false understanding by emphasizing the connection of Baptism and faith, and he especially undertakes to prove that infants *can* believe and so should be baptized.[6] Three years later, in his letter to two pastors *Concerning Rebaptism* (1528),[7] the structure of Luther's presentation was unclear—because he wrote it "briefly and hastily"[8]—but three main points appear: (1) No one should be rebaptized. (2) Baptism is objectively valid apart from faith. (3) Infants should be baptized.

In 1528, on the afternoons of each Sunday in February, Luther preached Baptism sermons in the style of catechetical sermons.[9] Luther's sermons were recorded by the deacon of the Wittenberg parish church, Georg Rörer (1492–1557), and should be compared with *Concerning Rebaptism*, which was being printed around the time that Luther preached these sermons.[10] On February 2, Luther emphasized the objectivity of Baptism based on God's command to baptize, an objectivity that remains even if the ministers who conduct the Baptisms or those who receive the Baptisms are bad people

---

[6] See below, pp. 3–12.

[7] AE 40:225–62.

[8] AE 40:261.

[9] Evidently Luther felt free to preach on the catechism, though Sunday afternoons were not necessarily established as times for catechism preaching at this time. In 1523 in Wittenberg, the Epistle reading of the Sunday was appointed to be preached at Vespers (see *Concerning the Order of Public Worship*, AE 53:13). By 1533, the Wittenberg church order specified that the early service on Sunday should include a sermon on the catechism, the sermon for the chief service was to be on the Gospel reading, and the ministers could use the Epistle or another text for the afternoon service (Sehling, *Die Evangelischen Kirchenordnungen*, 1.1:700–701).

[10] WA 27:32; AE 40:225–62.

or unbelievers. This is illustrated with numerous examples from God's other commands and institutions, all of which remain valid and real, even if they are misused.[11] The word Luther uses for "objectively valid" is usually the German word *recht*, which means not only "right" but also "real" or "true."[12] On February 9, speaking against Anabaptist claims that the unbelief or impiety of "Papist" priests made Roman Catholic Baptism unreal, Luther explained that Baptism, along with the Lord's Supper and the preaching of God's Word, were and are valid in the papacy, even though the pope is Antichrist. Certainty of salvation should not be placed on our own faith, but on God's command and order.[13] On February 16, Luther first argued that children *can* believe, especially on the basis of the example of John the Baptist leaping in the womb of his mother at the voice of Mary (Luke 1:44). Next, Luther argued that children do in fact believe, and he brought forward the parallel between New Testament Baptism and Old Testament circumcision as part of his proof. Moreover, children without the use of reason are the model believers. Christ is present in Baptism; He does the baptizing. Luther also included his historical arguments for Baptism here.[14] Finally, Luther rejected the notion that Baptism is merely a sign of already having been reborn.[15] On February 23, Luther dealt again with Baptism as "sign." If Baptism is called a "sign," it is not a sign of recognition among Christians, but a sign given by God to confirm faith and forgive sins. Luther listed many examples of signs from the Old Testament in which God worked to confirm faith. He also listed many New Testament passages that speak of Baptism's effects and "usefulness." Luther's main point here was that God works sacramentally through His chosen, physical, created things. In this sense, one may speak of Baptism as a "sign."[16] In the unpublished sermon series of 1528, 1531, and 1532, Luther began his sermon series by emphasizing the greatness of Baptism, since it was instituted by Christ. Although in each series he indicated that his next topic would be the effects of Baptism, in 1528 and 1532 Luther never got around to preaching on Baptism's effects.[17] Nevertheless, the 1528 sermons are especially rich and would be worthy objects of future research.

---

[11] Afternoon sermon of February 2, 1528, WA 27:32–38.

[12] See *DWB*, s.v. "recht" II.3.e.ι.

[13] Afternoon sermon of February 9, 1528, WA 27:41–45.

[14] See these arguments as classically formulated in the *Large Catechism* (1529) IV 49–51 (Kolb-Wengert, pp. 462–63; *Concordia*, p. 428).

[15] Afternoon sermon of February 16, 1528, WA 26:49–53.

[16] Afternoon sermon of February 23, 1528, WA 27:55–60.

[17] WA 26:60.27; 36:134.15.

By the advent of the *Small* and *Large Catechism* in 1529, Luther had refined the structure of his teaching: (1) The essence of Baptism is water with the Word of God. (2) The effects of Baptism. (3) The relation of Baptism and faith, with infant Baptism. (4) The ongoing effect or significance of Baptism (which might be called its ongoing sanctification aspect).

In January 1531, Luther preached three sermons on Baptism, with Georg Rörer again as his stenographer. On January 5, for the vigil of Epiphany, Luther read Matt. 3:13–17, the account of Christ's Baptism, as his sermon text. He stated that he wanted the lectionary to be changed, so that Christ's Baptism would always be treated on Epiphany. "This is the Gospel and text that ought to be read today, if it were to be ordered aright."[18] In that sermon and the next one, on the afternoon of January 6, Luther dealt with Christ's Baptism by John the Baptist and focused on Christ's person and work, though not much on the doctrine of Baptism itself.[19] On January 15, however, Luther gave an excellent treatment of the doctrine of Baptism, repeating most of the themes from the *Large Catechism* while adding a few new ones. He began by stating that it had been "ordered" (according to Rörer) or it was the "custom" (as Rörer later noted) that there be preaching on Baptism (namely, during the season of Epiphany), so Luther wanted to stay with this ordinance or custom.[20] In this sermon Luther preached the essence of Baptism as water with God's Word, the permanence of Baptism (similar but not identical to the Roman Catholic teaching of an indelible character), and the benefits of Baptism, which go beyond one-time purification of the soul.[21] This sermon of January 15 is especially rich. It, too, would be a worthy object of future study.

From January through March 1532, Luther preached four sermons on Baptism. Along with Georg Rörer, notes were taken by Anton Lauterbach (1502–69).[22] In this series, Luther mainly praises the greatness of Baptism. On the morning of January 14, Luther preached that Baptism is not just for

---

[18] *Hoc est Euangelium et textus, qui hodie debet legi, wens recht solt geordnet sein* (WA 34/1:24.6–7).

[19] Sermon of January 5 and afternoon sermon of January 6, 1531, WA 34/1:21–31, 42–50.

[20] WA 34/1:87.20 and apparatus on this line. On December 5, 1537, Luther preached that "our church order instructs us to preach on [the Sunday after Epiphany] about Baptism so that it is sustained within Christendom" (*Sermons on Matthew 18–24* [1537–40], AE 68:70). See above, p. xv n. 9.

[21] Sermon of January 15, 1531, WA 34/1:87–98.

[22] Sermons of January 14 (morning and afternoon), February 11, and March 10, 1532, WA 36:96–102, 102–10, 111–17, 126–34. Lauterbach's notes are indicated in the Weimar edition as "N." Lauterbach's notes on Luther's preaching are included in Codex Solger 13 of the City Library of Nürnberg, which bears marks of ownership by Friedrich Myconius (1490–1546) and Johann Aurifaber (1519–75). The identification of Lauterbach as the original

a moment, but it is an eternal, spiritual, heavenly "estate." As an estate, it surpasses monasticism and even marriage.[23] Luther's afternoon sermon for January 14 focused on the preaching and baptizing of John the Baptist. By preaching that all people had to be baptized, John demonstrated the greatness of Baptism and the pettiness of our works. Christ was baptized in order to confirm John's baptizing activity. The content of Mark 16:16 ("Whoever believes and is baptized shall be saved") is found already in John's preaching and baptizing.[24] In the sermons of February 11 and March 10, Luther stressed the greatness and necessity of Baptism.[25] The unique insights of the former two sermons, which are worthy candidates for future study, overshadow the frequently encountered admonitions of the latter two sermons.

Unlike the Baptism sermon series of 1528, 1531, and 1532, Luther's six Baptism sermons from 1534 were edited and published during his lifetime (in 1535). These sermons have been translated by Christopher Boyd Brown and Matthew Carver for the American edition of Luther's works and are included here.[26] They are excellent examples of Luther's preaching on Baptism. In these sermons, Luther structures his presentation in three parts: (1) the essence of Baptism is water, Word, and God's command; (2) the effects of Baptism; and (3) those who receive it (with faith or without). Here we see that Luther clarified the essence of Baptism as including not just the words of consecration for the baptismal water but also the institution and command of God to carry out this sacrament. We also see that Luther has simplified his structure by putting the significance of Baptism into the effects of Baptism (point 2) and the persons who receive Baptism (point 3). Christ's Baptism plays an important role here.

In January and February 1538, Luther preached six sermons on Baptism, recorded by Georg Rörer and Johann Stolz (ca. 1514–56).[27] After Luther's death, these sermons were edited by Johann Aurifaber for publication but

---

scribe is based on a comparison of the handwriting. See WA 27:xvii–xviii; 31/2:vii–viii; WA Br 14:116n.

[23] Sermon of January 14 (morning), 1532, WA 36:96–102.

[24] Sermon of January 14 (afternoon), 1532, WA 36:102–10.

[25] Sermons of February 11 and March 10, 1532, WA 36:111–17, 126–34.

[26] *Sermons on Holy Baptism*, Matt. 3:13–17 (January 18, 25; February 1, 2, 8, 22, 1534), AE 57:139–89; see below, pp. 13–59.

[27] Sermons of January 20, 27, February 10, 17, 24, and March 3, 1538, WA 46:145–51, 151–55, 167–73, 174–78, 179–85, 194–201. On Stolz, see the introduction by Christopher Boyd Brown, AE 58:xxiv–xxv; Reinhold Jauernig, "Johann Stoltz," in *Luther in Thüringen* (Berlin: Evangelische Verlagsanstalt, [1952]), pp. 229–37; cf. Luther's appraisal of him in WA Br 12:431, no. 4325.

were not published until the late 1800s.[28] They have been translated by Matthew Carver and are published here for the first time in English. Luther structured his teaching in these sermons as follows: (1) The sacraments are God's institution. (2) Baptism is based on God's command, not on our faith. (3) The essence of Baptism is water and God's Word. (4) The power of Baptism. (5) The Baptism of Christ. (6) Baptism is an everlasting covenant. Here we see that Luther continues to emphasize God's institution and command, but he has gone back to speaking about Baptism as being essentially the water with the Word of God. As in the 1534 sermon series, Christ's Baptism is important. In fact, it is in connection with the words of the Father to Christ—"This is My beloved Son" (Matt. 3:17)—that Luther explains Baptism as an eternal covenant.

In January 1539, Luther preached three sermons on Baptism, again recorded by Georg Rörer and Johann Stolz.[29] These, too, were edited by Johann Aurifaber for publication but remained unpublished until the early 1900s.[30] They have been translated by Matthew Carver and are published here for the first time in English. This year, for his last sermon series on Baptism, Luther used the same basic structure as the previous year. There are three parts: (1) Baptism is God's institution, based on His command, not on our faith. (2) Baptism is water and speaking the words "I baptize you in the name of the Father and of the Son and of the Holy Spirit." (3) The power of Baptism.

Johann Aurifaber's Editing of Luther's 1538 and 1539 Baptism Sermons

Johann Aurifaber was Luther's domestic assistant in the latter years of Luther's life. With Georg Rörer and Andreas Poach (1515–85), Aurifaber was an editor of the Jena edition of Luther's collected writings.[31] Aurifaber edited and published other writings of Luther, such as a collection of his

---

[28] E[2] 20/1:20–29, 29–37; Georg Buchwald, ed., *Ungedruckte Predigten D. Martin Luthers aus den Jahren 1537-1540: Zum ersten Mal veröffentlicht* (Leipzig: G. Strübigs Verlag, M. Altmann, 1905), pp. 283–88, 289–93, 293–300; E[2] 20/1:75–85. A sermon in E[2] 20/1:12–20 (Aland Pr 1692) is listed there as the first of four Baptism sermons, but it is not a Baptism sermon, and there were actually six (not four) Baptism sermons in that year's series.

[29] Sermons of January 6 (afternoon), January 19, and January 26, 1539, WA 47:640–46, 646–52, 653–59.

[30] Buchwald, *Ungedruckte Predigten*, pp. 500–514.

[31] *Der Erste [-achte] Teil aller Bücher vnd Schrifften des thewren/ seligen Mans Doct: Mart: Lutheri* (Jhena: Christian Rödinger, Donatus Richtzenhain, Thomas Rebart, 1555[–58]); *Tomvs primvs [-qvartvs] omnivm opervm Reuerendi Patris D. M. L.* (Ienae: Christian Rödinger, Donatus Richtzenhain, Thomas Rebart, 1556[–58]).

correspondence,[32] and, most famously, he edited Luther's *Table Talk* in a form that would become standard for Luther's published utterances at table until the publication of the Weimar edition.[33] Aurifaber also used Rörer's Latin-German stenographic notes to prepare a smooth German translation of many of Luther's sermons for publication in the Eisleben edition of Luther's writings (which was intended as an extension of the Wittenberg and Jena editions).[34] However, only two volumes of the Eisleben edition, including writings dated from 1516–37, were ever published. Chronologically, these Baptism sermons from 1538 and 1539 would have fit in the proposed third volume of the Eisleben edition, but despite Aurifaber's editorial work, they were not brought to the press until his work was rediscovered and published in the latter part of the nineteenth century.[35] These Baptism sermons, with many others from this time period (1537–40), were first published by Georg Buchwald, who did not hazard a guess as to Aurifaber's original publishing plans for this material.[36]

Aurifaber's editing is a creditable attempt to take Rörer's sometimes fragmentary bilingual notes and make them legible for readers. Bible passage incipits in Rörer are filled out by Aurifaber. All the Latin is translated into German. Occasionally words are added to clarify or to repeat a subject that had been omitted by Rörer. For example, where Rörer had "time determined, when He would come," Aurifaber gives: "and the time had been

---

[32] Luther, *Epistolarvm Reverendi Patris Domini D. Martini Lutheri, Tomus primus*, ed. Johann Aurifaber (Jena: Christian Rödinger, 1556); *Secundvs Tomvs epistolarvm Reuerendi patris Domini Doctoris Martini Lvtheri* (Eisleben: Andreas Petri, 1565). See Robert Kolb, *Martin Luther as Prophet, Teacher, and Hero: Images of the Reformer, 1520–1620*, Texts and Studies in Reformation and Post-Reformation Thought (Grand Rapids: Baker Books, 1999), p. 151.

[33] Johann Aurifaber, ed., *Tischreden Oder Colloqvia Doct. Mart: Luthers/ So er in vielen Jaren/ gegen gelarten Leuten/ auch frembden Gesten/ vnd seinen Tischgesellen gefüret/ Nach den Heubtstücken vnserer Christlichen Lere/ zusammen getragen* (Eisleben: Urban Gaubisch, 1566); Martin Luther, *Tischreden Oder Colloquia, so Er in Vielen Jahren Gegen Gelahrte Leuten, Auch Fremden Gästen und Seinen Tischgesellen Geführet: Nach Aurifaber's Erster Ausgabe*, ed. Eduard Förstemann and Heinrich Ernst Bindseil (Leipzig: Gebauersche Buchhandlung, 1844–48); Martin Luther, *D. Martin Luthers Werke: Tischreden*, 6 vols. (Weimar: H. Böhlau, 1912–21). See Kolb, *Martin Luther as Prophet, Teacher, and Hero*, pp. 152–54; and the introduction by Christopher Boyd Brown to *Sixteenth-Century Biographies of Martin Luther*, Luther's Works Companion Volume (St. Louis: Concordia, 2018), pp. xviii–xix and the notes there.

[34] *Der Erste [und Ander] Theil Der Bücher/ Schrifften/ vnd Predigten des Ehrwirdigen Herrn/ D. Martin Luthers deren viel weder in den Wittenbergischen noch Jhenischen Tomis zufinden* (Eisleben: Urban Gaubisch, 1564[–65]).

[35] See the introduction by Christopher Boyd Brown, AE 58:xxvi–xxvii; Kolb, *Martin Luther as Prophet, Teacher, and Hero*, 150; Eike Wolgast and Hans Volz, "Geschichte der Luther-Ausgaben vom 16. bis zum 19. Jahrhundert," WA 60:547–48.

[36] Buchwald, *Ungedruckte Predigten*, [iii].

named, when *this Seed, the Savior of the world,* would come."[37] The text in italics was added, drawn from the context, to fill out the meaning.

On another occasion, Aurifaber expands and adds clarification that is based on the context. Rörer had: "Here, first, pertains and is of import especially that no one should think a human thing, that Baptism [was] thought up from human will."[38] On its own, this makes sense in context, but Aurifaber expands it to make the topic more clear. Perhaps Aurifaber was also reading the *ut* clause (translated above as "that") as a purpose or result clause, rather than a German nominal *dass* clause. Aurifaber gives: "Now much depends on this, that we first know from where Baptism comes, so that no one would think that it is something human or that Baptism was thought up, invented from human will."[39]

An especially creditable example of Aurifaber's modest expansions is seen in this short Rörer text: "Whoever thus, is in error and goes to the devil. Pope indulgence, purgatory."[40] Aurifaber gives: ". . . for whoever sees it as that, he is in error and goes to the devil, as the pope does, too, with his indulgence and purgatory."[41]

Often Rörer leaves out Luther's words, indicating omissions with the mark "&c." In these cases, Aurifaber often draws on the context to supply the missing words. Rörer had: "They go off in houses, in the state and make laws, etc. But in the church . . ."[42] Aurifaber gives: "They go off in houses and in the worldly governance and make laws and order, territorial law and custom; *that can be allowed.* But in the Church of God . . ."[43]

Occasionally, if Aurifaber could not decipher Rörer's notes, he omitted a phrase. For example, Rörer wrote: "*Invocatus S excog,*" which the editors of the Weimar edition have expanded to "*Invocatus S[anctus] excog[itatus],*"

[37] Rörer: *Tempus determinatum, quando venturus* (WA 46:145.21). Aurifaber: ". . . und ist die Zeit ernennet worden, wenn dieser Same, der Welt Heiland, kommen würde" (E² 20/1:21.33–35). See below, p. 62.

[38] *Huc 1. pertinet et refert maxime, ut nemo putet humanam rem, quod baptismus ex voluntate humana excogitatus* (WA 46:146.7–8).

[39] *Doran liegt nun viel, daß wir erstlich wissen, woher die Taufe kompt, auf daß niemands gedenke, daß es ein menschlich Ding sei oder daß die Taufe aus menschlichem Willen erdacht erfunden sei* (E² 20/1:22.17–21). Cf. below, p. 62.

[40] *Qui ita, ist irr und geht zu dem Teufel zu* (WA 46:146.10).

[41] *. . . denn wer es dafür ansiehet, der ist irre und gehet dem Teufel zu, wie denn der Papst mit seinem Ablaß und Fegfeuer auch thut* (E² 20/1:22.24–27). Cf. below, pp. 62–63.

[42] *Sie gehen hin in domibus, in pol[itia] und machen leges &c. Sed in Ecclesia . . .* (WA 46:146.24–25).

[43] *Sie gehen hin in Häusern und im weltlichem Regiment, und machen Gesetze und Ordnung, Landrecht und Gewohnheit; das laß man also hinpassieren. Aber in der Kirchen Gottes . . .* (E² 20/1:23.14–17). Cf. below, p. 63.

which translates literally to "invoked saint thought up"—a meaningless phrase. Rörer probably meant: "He thought up the invocation of the saints." Aurifaber simply omitted this in his adaptation.[44]

Sometimes Aurifaber changes the sense of the words recorded by Rörer. For example, where Rörer wrote "[Christ would] have the damage,"[45] Aurifaber gave "[Christ would] heal the damage."[46] Instead of Rörer's word "absolution," Aurifaber gives "confession."[47] Instead of Rörer's word "preaching," Aurifaber gives "preaching office."[48]

As a result perhaps of little changes such as these, older scholarship questioned the reliability of Aurifaber's editing in presenting Luther's own words and thoughts. More recent scholarship, however, has viewed Aurifaber as a careful and faithful editor of Luther, a view with which we wholly agree. While the text that Aurifaber gave may not be Luther's words at every point, it is probably the best overall interpretation of Rörer's difficult stenography that one could possibly have.[49] Aurifaber's editing is creditable, trustworthy, equal to or surpassing the work of modern translators of Rörer's stenographic notes, and surpassing them all in his proximity to the man who was preaching and to the great events of the sixteenth century.

Now published in English translation for the first time, these sermons edited by Aurifaber present a unique opportunity to read Luther's baptismal preaching as Luther would have wanted it published.[50]

B.T.G.M.

---

[44] WA 46:146.10; E² 20/1:22.

[45] *den schaden haben* (WA 46:145.18).

[46] *den Schaden heilen* (E² 20/1:21.26).

[47] *absolutionem* (WA 46:146.21–22); *Beichte* (E² 20/1:23.10).

[48] *praedicationis* (WA 46:145.24); *Predigtampt* (E² 20/1:22.3). But nearby, Aurifaber translates *ministerii* also as *Predigtampt.*

[49] Gustav Kawerau, "Zur Frage nach der Zuverlässigkeit Johannes Aurifabers als Sammlers und Herausgebers Lutherischer Schriften," *ARG* 12 (1915): 155–57; Otto Clemen, "Johannes Aurifaber als gewerbsmäßiger Hersteller von Lutherhandschriften," *ARG* 29 (1932): 85–96; Helmar Junghans, "Aurifaber, Johannes," *TRE* 4:752–55.

[50] Luther worked with a team of editors during his lifetime and expected that they would improve and smooth out his sometimes ad hoc sermons. See the introduction by Benjamin T. G. Mayes to the *Church Postil* (1540–44), AE 75:xiii–xxxi; and the introduction by Christopher Boyd Brown to Aurifaber's edition of Luther's sermons on Matthew 18–24, AE 68:xiii–xviii.

MARTIN LUTHER
ON HOLY BAPTISM

CHAPTER ONE

INFANT BAPTISM AND FAITH THAT IS NOT ONE'S OWN (1525)

Because[1] the season and this Gospel[2] present it, we must say a little about faith that is not one's own[3] and its power, since many are concerned about this, especially for the sake of young children, whom people think are saved in Baptism not through their own but through another person's faith. Here this servant became healthy not through his own faith but through the faith of his master. We have never yet treated this matter; therefore, we must treat it here in order to prevent, as much we can, future danger and error.[4]

First, we must have the foundation firm and certain that no one is saved by another person's faith or righteousness, but through his own. On the other hand, no one is condemned for another person's unbelief or sins, but for his own unbelief, as the Gospel clearly and plainly says: "Whoever believes and is baptized will be saved, but whoever does not believe will be condemned" (Mark 16 [:16]). [Paul writes]: "The righteous shall live by his faith" (Romans 1 [:17]). [Christ says]: "Whoever believes in Him will not perish but has eternal life" [John 3:16]. Again: "Whoever believes in Him will not be judged, but whoever does not believe is judged already" (John 3 [:18]).

These are clear and open words that each must believe for himself, and he cannot be helped by another person's faith without his own faith. We

[1] Translated by James L. Langebartels from E[2] 11:60–73 and WA 17/2:78–88, a part of Luther's *Church Postil* (1540–44), sermon for Epiphany 3 on Matt. 8:1–13. This translation originally appeared in AE 76:257–66; the annotations have been amended for inclusion here.

[2] The Gospel reading was Matt. 8:1–13 (AE 76:251).

[3] *von dem frembden Glauben*

[4] Compare the different approaches to the question of whether one may be saved by the faith of another in *Defense and Explanation of All the Articles* (1521), AE 32:14; sermon for Trinity 12 on Mark 7:31–37, paragraph 11, in Roth's edition of the *Summer Postil* (1526), Lenker 4:375 (WA 10/1.2:353–55), based on a sermon of September 7, 1522 (WA 10/3:304–12); and *Comfort for Women Who Have Had a Miscarriage* (1542), AE 43:247–48.

must not yield these passages or deny them, no matter what happens; we should first let all the world be destroyed before we change this divine truth. If something is brought up which seems to be against this and which you do not know how to answer, you should confess that you do not understand it and leave it to God, rather than admit something against these clear passages. Let Gentiles, Jews, Turks, little children, and everything remain what it is and where it can, but these words should and must be right and true.

Now the question is where the young children remain who do not yet have reasoning abilities and cannot believe for themselves, because it is written: "Faith comes through hearing, and hearing through the preaching of God's Word" (Romans 10 [:17]). [Some say that] young children neither hear nor understand God's Word, and therefore they cannot have their own faith.

The sophists in the universities and the pope's rabble have invented the following answer to the question: "Young children are baptized without their own faith, namely, on the faith of the Church, which the sponsors confess at the Baptism. Accordingly, in Baptism sins are forgiven for the child from the power and might of Baptism, and its own faith is poured in with grace, so that it becomes a newborn child through water and the Holy Spirit [John 3:5]."

But if you ask them for the basis of this answer and where this is in Scripture, then it is found up the dark chimney,[5] or they point to their cardinal's hat and say: "We are the highly learned doctors, and we say so; therefore, it is true, and you dare not ask any more about it." Nearly all their doctrine has no other basis than their own dreams and opinions. When they most specially arm themselves [with proof], then they drag in by the hair some passage from St. Augustine or another holy father. But that is not enough for us in these matters which concern the soul's salvation. They themselves and all the holy fathers are people and human beings. Who will guarantee and provide surety that they are speaking correctly? Who will rely on that and die for it, since they speak without Scripture or God's Word? As for the saints, here they don't matter—when it means losing or preserving my soul eternally, I cannot rely on all the angels and saints, to say nothing of one or two saints, if they do not show me God's Word.

From these lies they have advanced and come so far that they have taught and still hold that the Sacraments have such power that even if you have no faith and receive the Sacrament (as long as you do not have the intention of sinning), then you obtain grace and the forgiveness of sins

[5] *Rauchloch*, i.e., it is found nowhere; cf. AE 37:242 n. 121; 60:162–63 n. 21.

without any faith.[6] They have introduced this from the previous opinion, namely, their dream that young children receive grace without any faith only from the might and power of Baptism. That is why they ascribe the same thing to adults and all people, because they are speaking these things out of their own heads. In that way they root out Christian faith in a masterful way, destroy it, and make it unnecessary; with the power of the Sacraments they establish only our own works. I have written enough about this in the article on the bull of Leo.[7]

The holy ancient fathers have spoken somewhat more about this, though not clearly enough. They do not speak about this imaginary power of the Sacraments; rather, they speak as if the young children were baptized in the faith of the Christian Church. But because they do not explain thoroughly how this Christian faith benefits the children, whether they receive their own faith through it or whether they are only baptized on the Christian faith, without their own faith, the sophists have gone ahead and explained the words of the holy fathers to mean that children are baptized without their own faith and receive grace only in the Church's faith. They are enemies of faith; if only they can elevate works, then faith must endure it. They do not once think that the holy fathers might have erred or that they themselves have incorrectly understood the fathers.

Guard yourself against this poison and error, even if it were the explicit opinion of all the fathers and councils; for it does not last, there is no basis in Scripture for it, but only the human opinions and dreams. Moreover, it is directly and openly against the chief passage, where Christ says, "Whoever believes and is baptized," etc. [Mark 16:16]. In short, the conclusion is that Baptism helps no one and is to be given to no one unless he believes for himself; without faith no one is to be baptized. St. Augustine himself says, "It is not the Sacrament which justifies, but faith in the Sacrament."[8]

Besides these there are some others, called the Waldensians,[9] who hold that each one must believe for himself and must receive Baptism or the

---

[6] Luther refers to the scholastic doctrine that the sacraments were effective "just by doing the work" (*ex opere operato*), regardless of the faith or merit of the minister and regardless of the faith or preparation of the recipient, provided only that the minister intended to perform a sacrament of the church and that the recipient did not willfully impose an obstacle to the sacrament. See Heiko A. Oberman, *The Harvest of Medieval Theology: Gabriel Biel and Late Medieval Nominalism*, 3rd ed. (Durham, NC: Labyrinth, 1983), pp. 146–60, 467.

[7] *Against the Bull of the Antichrist* (1520), WA 6:597–629; cf. Brecht 1:409–12.

[8] *Non sacramentum justificat, sed fides sacramenti*. On the origin of this phrase and its attribution to Augustine (345–430), see Karl-Heinz zur Mühlen, "Zur Rezeption der Augustinischen Sakramentsformel," *Zeitschrift für Theologie und Kirche* 70 (1973): 50–76.

[9] Luther often called the Bohemian Brethren or Unity of Brethren "Waldensians." Cf. Luther's preface to *Account of the Faith of the Brethren* (1533), AE 60:17–23; and preface to

Sacrament with his own faith; if he does not, then for him Baptism or the Sacrament is good for nothing. So far they speak and teach correctly. But when they go ahead and nevertheless baptize young children whom they regard as not having their own faith, that is a mockery of holy Baptism, and they sin against the Second Commandment when they consciously and wantonly take God's name and Word unnecessarily and in vain. There is no help for them in their excuse that children are baptized on the basis of their future faith, when they will think for themselves. Faith must be present before or in Baptism; otherwise the child is not freed from the devil and sins.

Therefore, if their opinion were correct, then everything that is done with the child in Baptism would have to be mere lies and mockery. The baptizer asks whether the child believes, and people answer for the child: "Yes." He asks whether [the child] wants to be baptized, and people answer for the child: "Yes." Nevertheless, no one is baptized for the child, but [the child] himself is baptized. Therefore, [the child] must himself believe, or the sponsors must be lying when they say in his place: "I believe." Likewise, the baptizer declares that [the child] is born anew, has forgiveness of sins, is freed from the devil, and as a sign of this he puts on him a white shirt and treats him in all things as a new, holy child of God. All of that would have to be false if his own faith were not there. It would be better never to baptize children than to act foolishly and deceptively with God's Word and Sacrament, as if He were an idol or a fool.

It also does not help that they divide the kingdom of God into three parts: first, the Christian Church; second, eternal life; third, the Gospel. Then they say that children are baptized into the kingdom of heaven in the third and first ways; that is, they are baptized not to be saved and to have the forgiveness of sins, but they are received into Christendom and brought to the Gospel. All of this is saying nothing and is invented out of their own opinions. It is not coming into the kingdom of heaven when I come among Christians and hear the Gospel. Even heathen can do that, even without Baptism. It is not coming into the kingdom of heaven when you say about the kingdom of heaven in the first, second, or third ways whatever you want; rather, being in the kingdom of heaven means that I am a living member of Christendom, and not only hear the Gospel but also believe it. Otherwise a man would be in the kingdom of heaven in the same way that I might throw a stick or a log among Christians, or as the devil is among them. Therefore, that [way of being among the Christians] is worthless.

It also follows from this that the Christian Church would have to have two kinds of Baptism, and that children would not have the same Baptism

---

Confession of the Barons and Nobles of Bohemia (1538), AE 60:214–19. With this title Luther also could be referring to Anabaptists.

as adults. Nevertheless, St. Paul says there is only "one Baptism, one Lord, one faith" (Ephesians 4 [:5]). If Baptism does not do and give to children what it does and gives to adults, then it is not the same Baptism; indeed, it is no Baptism, but playing at and mocking Baptism, since there is no other Baptism than that which saves [cf. 1 Pet. 3:21]. If you know or believe that it does not save, then you should not give it; but if you do give it, then you do not give Christian Baptism, for you do not believe that it accomplishes what Baptism should accomplish. Therefore, it is a different and foreign baptism. For that reason it would almost be necessary for the Waldensians to have themselves baptized again, as they baptize our people again, because they not only received Baptism without faith but even against faith.[10] In mockery and dishonor of God they give a different, foreign, unchristian baptism.

If we cannot answer this question better and prove that young children themselves believe and have their own faith, then it is my sincere counsel and judgment that we immediately desist—the sooner the better—and never baptize a child, so that we do not mock and slander the blessed majesty of God with such tomfoolery and trickery which has nothing behind it.

Therefore, we here speak plainly and conclude that in Baptism the children themselves believe and have their own faith, which God works in them when the sponsors intercede for them and bring them into the faith of the Christian Church. We call that "the power of someone else's faith":[11] not that anyone can be saved by that [kind of faith], but that through it, as through its intercession and help, he can himself obtain from God his own faith by which he is saved.

It happens the same way as my natural living and dying. If I am to live, then I must myself be born, and no one can be born for me so that I live through them; however, my mother and the midwife can through their living help me to my birth, so that I live in that way. So if I am to die, then I must myself suffer death, and no one can die for me so that I die; but he can certainly help me to my own death, such as when he frightens me, falls on me, chokes or crushes me, or suffocates me with stench. Likewise, no one can go into hell for me; but he can mislead me by false doctrine and life, so that I go into [hell] by my own error, brought onto me by his error. So no one can go to heaven for me; but he can help me to get there by preaching, teaching, governing, praying, and obtaining faith from God [for me], through which I can go to heaven. This centurion was not healed of the paralysis of his servant, but he acquired having his servant obtain health.

So here we also say that children are not baptized in the faith of the sponsors or of the Church, but the faith of sponsors and of the Church

---

[10] See *Concerning Rebaptism* (1528), AE 40:229–62.

[11] *die Kraft des frembden Glaubens*

prays for and gains for them their own faith in which they are baptized and believe for themselves. We have strong and firm passages about that (Matthew 19 [:13–15]; Mark 10 [:13–16]; Luke 18 [:15–16]). When some brought little children to the Lord Jesus so that He could touch them and the disciples hindered them, He rebuked the disciples, embraced the children, laid His hands on them, blessed them, and said, "To such belongs the kingdom of God" [Matt. 19:14; Mark 10:14; Luke 18:16]. No one will take these passages away from us nor overcome them with good reasons. It says here that Christ does not want people to forbid the little children to be brought to Him; He even commands that they be brought to Him, blesses them, and gives them the kingdom of heaven. Let us note that well.

Without a doubt this was written about natural children, and it is wrong when people want to explain Christ's words as if He had meant spiritual children, who are small because of their humility. These were bodily small children, whom Luke calls "infants" [Luke 18:15]. On them His blessing was placed, and about them He says that the kingdom of heaven is theirs. What do we want to say here? Do we want to say that they were without their own faith and that the other passage is false: "Whoever does not believe will be condemned" [Mark 16:16]? Then Christ is also lying or dissembling when He says that the kingdom of heaven is theirs, and is not speaking seriously about the true kingdom of heaven.

Interpret these words of Christ as you please, we have [to conclude] that children are to be brought to Christ and are not to be hindered; when they are brought to Him, then He compels us to believe that He blesses them and gives them the kingdom of heaven, as He does for these children. It is proper for us to act and believe in no other way, as long as the words stand: "Let the little children come to Me and do not hinder them" [Matt. 19:14]. No less is it proper for us to believe that when they are brought to Him, He will embrace them, lay His hands on them, bless them, and give them heaven, as long as this text stands that He blessed and gave heaven to the children who were brought to Him. Who can ignore this text? Who, on the other hand, will be so bold as not to allow little children to come to Baptism or not to believe that He blesses them when they come to Him?

He is just as present in Baptism now as He was then. Because we Christians certainly know this, we dare not keep Baptism away from children. So also we dare not doubt that He blesses all who come to Him, just as He blessed those [children]. Thus nothing more remains than the thoughts and faith of those who brought the little children to Him. By bringing them, they cause and help the little children to be blessed and to obtain the kingdom of heaven, [but] that could not be if [the children] did not have their own faith for themselves, as has been said.[12]

So we also say here that the little children are brought to Baptism by the faith and work of another; but when they get there and the priest or baptizer deals with them in Christ's place, then He blesses them and gives them faith and the kingdom of heaven, for the priest's word and deed are the word and work of Christ Himself.

St. John also agrees with this when he says: "I am writing to you, fathers"; "I am writing to you, young men"; "I am writing to you, children" (1 John 2 [:13]). He is not satisfied to write to the young men; he also writes to the children—and writes that they know the Father. From this it follows that the apostles also baptized children and held the view that they believe and know the Father, just as if they had begun to reason and could read. Although someone could explain the word "children" as referring to the adults, as Christ sometimes calls His disciples [e.g., John 13:33], yet here it is certain that he is speaking about those who are younger than the young men, so that it sounds like he is speaking about the young crowd, those who are under fifteen or eighteen years, and excludes nobody down to the first year, for all these are called "children."

But we want to look at their reason for thinking that the children do not believe. They say that it is because they have not yet begun to reason and so cannot hear God's Word; but where God's Word is not heard, there can be no faith: "Faith comes from hearing, and hearing comes from God's Word" (Romans 10 [:17]). Tell me, is it Christian to judge God's works according to our opinion and to say, "Children have not begun to reason, and therefore they could not believe"? How is it, then, that through your own reasoning you have already come away from faith, and the children by their unreasoning have come to faith?

Dear friend, what good does reason do for faith and God's Word? Is it not [reason] which most strongly opposes faith and the Word of God, so that no one can come to faith because of [reason]? It will not tolerate God's Word unless it is blinded and disgraced, so that we must die to [reason] and become fools, as unreasonable and unwise as a little child, before we believe and receive God's grace. Christ says: "Unless you turn and become like children, you will never enter the kingdom of heaven" (Matthew 18 [:3]). How often does Christ tell us that we must become children and fools? How often does He condemn reason?

Likewise, tell me what kind of reason the little children had whom Christ embraced and blessed and to whom He gave heaven? Were they not still without reason? Why, then, does He command them to be brought to

---

[12] See above, pp. 7–8.

Him and bless them? Where did they get the faith which makes them children of the kingdom of heaven? Yes, just because they are without reason and foolish, they are better adapted for faith than adults and the wise, for whom reason is always in the way and refuses to push its big head through the narrow door. If we are talking here about faith and God's work, then we must not look at reason or its works. Here God works alone, and reason is dead, blind, and like a stupid log in this work, so that Scripture is right when it says, "God is astonishing in His saints" [cf. Ps. 68:35 (67:36 Vg)]. Likewise: "As the heavens are higher than the earth, so are My ways higher than your ways and My thoughts than your thoughts" (Isaiah 55 [:9]).

But since they are stuck so deep in their reason, we must attack them with their own cleverness. Tell me, why do you baptize a person when he has begun to reason? You answer: "He hears God's Word and believes." I ask: How do you know that? You say, "He confesses it with his mouth." What shall I say? What if he lies and deceives? You cannot see his heart. Well, then, you baptize on no other basis than what the man shows outwardly. You are uncertain of his faith and must think that if he does not have more on the inside in his heart than you perceive on the outside, then his hearing, his confessing, and his faith will not help, for it may be sheer delusion and not true faith. Who are you, then, to say that external hearing and confessing are necessary for Baptism? [You say that] where these are not, we should not baptize, and where they are, we should baptize. But here you yourself confess that such hearing and confessing are uncertain and are not enough for a person to receive Baptism. Why do you baptize? How will you continue, when you have so thrown Baptism into doubt?

Is it not true that you must come and say that it is improper for you to do or know any more than that you should baptize whoever is brought to you and asks for Baptism? You must believe or commit to God whether or not he inwardly, truly believes; in that way you are excused and baptize correctly. Why, then, will you not do that for the children, whom Christ commands to be brought to Him and whom He wants to bless? Rather, you first want to have the outward hearing and confessing, which you confess is uncertain and insufficient for the Baptism of the one to be baptized. You abandon the sure words of Christ (when He commands that little children be brought to Him) for the sake of your uncertain external hearing.

Moreover, tell me, where is the reason of a person who believes in Christ while he is asleep, since his faith and God's grace never leave him? If faith can remain without the help of reason, so that [reason] is unaware of it, then why should [faith] not also begin in children before reason knows anything about it? I could say the same thing about all the estates in which a Christian lives and is busy or otherwise occupied, that he is unaware of his faith and reason, and yet his faith does not on that account cease. God's works are secret and wonderful, where and when He wants; on the other hand, they are quite obvious, where and when He wants, so that they are too high and too deep for us to judge about them.

Because He commands us here not to hinder little children from coming to Him so that He may bless them, and we are not required to be certain about the internal state of faith (external hearing and confessing are not enough for the one baptized), we are to be content that, for us who are doing the baptizing, it is enough to hear the confession of those to be baptized, who themselves come to us. [We are to hear their confession] so that we do not give the Sacrament against our conscience to those from whom no fruit is to be expected. But when they assure our conscience with their seeking and confessing that we may give it to them as a Sacrament which gives grace, then we are excused. If his faith is not true, we leave that to God; we have not given it as a useless thing, but with the consciousness that it is beneficial.

I say all of this so that we do not baptize thoughtlessly, as those do who give it with wanton knowledge that it does nothing and is not beneficial. Those baptizers sin by deliberately using God's Sacrament and Word in a useless way, or consciously thinking that it cannot do anything. That is treating the Sacrament in an unworthy way; it tempts and slanders God. That is not giving the Sacrament but mocking the Sacrament. But if the person baptized lies and does not believe—well, you have still done right and have given the true Sacrament with a good conscience, as something that ought to be useful.

As for those who do not come of themselves but are brought (as Christ commands us to bring the little children [Matt. 19:14]), you should commit their faith to Him who commands us to bring them and baptize them on His command, and say: "Lord, You bring them here and command me to baptize them, so You will certainly answer for them. I rely on that. I dare not drive them away or hinder them." If they have not heard the Word, by which faith comes, as adults hear it, they hear it like little children. Adults grasp [the Word] with their ears and reason, [but] often without faith. [Little children] hear it with their ears, without reason and with faith. Faith is all the closer the less reason there is. [The faith] which brings them is stronger than the will of adults who come of themselves.

What troubles these writers most is that in adults there is reason, which acts as if it believes the Word it hears; they call that "believing." On the other hand, they see that in children there is as yet no reason, for they act as if they do not believe. But they do not see that faith in God's Word is a much different and deeper thing than what reason does with God's Word. [Faith] is God's work alone beyond all reason. The child is closer than the adult—yes, much closer—and the adult is farther away than the child—yes, much farther away.

But this is a human work, made by reason. It seems to me that if any Baptism is certain, the Baptism of children should be most certain, just because of the words of Christ telling us to bring them, while the adults come on their own. There can be deception in adults because of their reason, but there can be no deception in children because their reason is hidden. Christ makes His blessing effective in them, as He has commanded that they be brought to Him. These very striking words are not to be disregarded, when He tells us to bring the children to Him and rebukes those who hinder it [Matt. 19:14].

But in so doing we do not want the preaching office weakened or set aside. To be sure, God does not have these things preached for the sake of rational hearing, since no fruit comes from that, but for the sake of spiritual hearing, which, as was said,[13] children also have, as well as and even better than adults. So they, too, indeed hear the Word. What else is Baptism than the Gospel to which they are brought? Even if they only hear it once, they hear it all the more powerfully because Christ, who has commanded them to be brought, welcomes them. The adults have the advantage here in that they hear it often and can reflect back on it. Nevertheless, it also happens with adults that even many sermons do not penetrate to spiritual hearing; but then it may hit home once in one sermon, and he has enough forever. What he hears afterward either improves what he heard first or destroys it again.

In summary, the Baptism and comfort of children is in these words: "Let the children come to Me; do not hinder them, for of such is the kingdom of God" [Mark 10:14]. He has said this and does not lie. So it must be right and Christian to bring little children to Him. That cannot happen other than in Baptism. So it must also be certain that He blesses them and gives the kingdom of heaven to all who come to Him, as the words read: "Of such is the kingdom of God." That is enough about this for now.

---

[13] See above, pp. 9–11.

CHAPTER TWO

SERMONS ON HOLY BAPTISM (1534)

PREFACE[1]

If I were to consider how much I have ingratiated myself until now with the beautiful, dear bride of the devil (which translated is "the world"), I would surely abandon my preaching and writing and wish that my name might be forgotten or never remembered rather than that I should keep on writing and preaching. For my part, that would be easy to do.

But since that gallant groom and his lovely bride are set on being feared and on gobbling up my Lord Jesus Christ, I must act as though I were afraid and as though my Lord Christ were dead and had rotted away fifteen hundred years ago—yet so that my fear is not unto death nor my Lord Christ's dying of harm to His life. For moderation (I hear it said) is good in all things.[2] Therefore, in order that my Lord Christ may not be so completely dead, and that I may not give up hope so utterly, I have seen fit to have these sermons of mine published in honor of holy Baptism. In our day this cannot but have many enemies, and the devil together with his world rages right against it.

Anabaptists are newly arisen, and going mad right along with them are the anti-Christian, ancient archanabaptists, who have baptized themselves with their own works and are still doing so. In the third place, the Epicureans are making incursions with a special mode of baptizing (which amounts to nothing).[3] Holy Baptism is being attacked so fiercely on every side that it is necessary for us to take heed and be vigilant.

[1] Translated by Christopher Boyd Brown and Matthew Carver from WA 37:627–72. This translation originally appeared in AE 57:141–89; the annotations have been amended for inclusion here.

[2] *masse ist . . . jnn allen dingen gut.* This saying is attested in Wander 3:490, "Mass" no. 54.

[3] Epicurus (341–270 BC) advocated an ethic of hedonism framed in metaphysical materialism. Although the "mode of baptizing" (affusion or sprinkling vs. immersion) was not a major

Although this might not pass without harm, I am still confident that the poor, insignificant Christ Jesus will hold the field against the devil and all his mighty men, scholars, and advisers. Whoever would be a faithful member of the despised, glorious King who must live forever, let him pray for these things with me now and that the time of His judgment and visitation, along with His kingdom, would come soon. To Him, our true, eternal God and Lord, with the Father and the Holy Spirit, be thanks and praise to eternity. Amen.

Gospel of Matthew 3 [:13–17]

> At that time, Jesus came from Galilee to the Jordan to John, that He might be baptized by him. But John prevented Him and said, "I have need to be baptized by You, and do You come to me?" But Jesus answered and said, "For now let it be so. Thus it is fitting for us to fulfill all righteousness." Then he permitted Him.
>
> And when Jesus was baptized, He went up at once out of the water. And behold, heaven opened above Him. And John saw the Spirit of God like a dove descend and come upon Him. And behold, a voice from heaven said, "This is My dear Son in whom I am well pleased."

On Holy Baptism by Dr. Martin Luther

This[4] is one of the chief festivals of the Lord Christ. In Greek it is called *Epiphania Domini*,[5] the "Appearing" or "Revealing of the Lord." It was named this and instituted by the ancient, holy fathers for three reasons: it celebrates, first, how Christ was revealed to the Gentiles from the East (who are called the Magi) through the star (Matthew 2 [:2]); second, how He did His first sign, turning water into wine at the wedding at Cana and revealing His glory to His disciples (John 2 [:11]); third, how He was baptized by John in the Jordan, and a glorious revelation from heaven took place over Him (Matthew 3 [:13–17]). There is without doubt good reason that a special time of year was first appointed in Christendom for preaching about the most worthy Sacrament of Holy Baptism, in order that it might be well-known to Christians and rightly honored as their highest treasure on earth, in which their salvation and blessedness are found. It is proper that

---

issue for most early Anabaptists, by the early 1530s there were some voices, including Michael Servetus (1511–53), who insisted on immersion as the only valid form. See George Huntston Williams, *The Radical Reformation*, 3rd ed. (Kirksville, MO: Truman State University Press, 2000), pp. 450–57.

[4] The first part of this printed sermon is a free adaptation of Rörer's notes of Luther's sermons on Baptism in 1534 (WA 37:258–67, 270–75, 278–84, 288–93, 299–304).

[5] In the words *Epiphania Domini*, the first is a latinized Greek word (from ἐπιφανεία), but the second is actually Latin. In Greek it would be ἐπιφανεία τοῦ κυρίου.

this festival should have the chief name of the Baptism of Christ, and this sermon on holy Baptism should emphasize this.[6]

For it is clearly not only proper and right but also of great necessity that this holy Sacrament should be discussed in Christendom and that people should be well instructed so that they do not despise their Baptism, as, unfortunately, has been the case. Until recently, nothing was being preached or taught about it, with the result that people paid no attention to Baptism, but put it behind them and almost completely forgot about it. Our own human works and various [monastic] orders were set up and put in its place, until finally things got so bad that a shabby monk's cowl was exalted and prized far above Baptism. This certainly would not have happened, and no doubt all kinds of abomination and error would have been avoided, if Christians had had their Baptism presented and portrayed to them rightly.

But the wretched devil had to work his heartache by stripping the pulpit of the true, pure doctrine and replacing it with his lies and deceptions. Moreover, God's Word and work always has this fortune in the world: what He says and does is regarded as worthless. But whatever the devil says and does it regards and esteems as precious. The Lord certainly encountered this in all His words and works. Therefore, He, our dear God, certainly needs His Word and works to be praised and emphasized for Christians in the best way possible so that they learn to regard them as great and splendid and do not act according to the judgment and opinion of the world.

For it is indeed true that in appearance [God's Word and work] are very insignificant and despicable because they are not produced and portrayed with great pomp and majesty. But if He adorned it with pure gold, pearls, silk, and satin; or had sacks full of gold and silver scattered about; or had it taught by great, powerful, highly learned men, rulers, and princes, it would have such prestige and honor that all the world would run to it and sing and talk about it. Now, however, because He offers it in such an insignificant way and without any pomp, only through one insignificant person's mouth and hand and with such an ordinary sign (water), it must be despised and rejected.

The world will and can esteem nothing that does not make the eyes stare and the mouth gape. "What can that be" (the world says), "that someone dips a child into water or pours out a handful upon it? What more is it than any other water used to wash the feet?" Now, that would be something if a priest came with precious malmsey or balsam, whereof one drop

[6] The following section is adapted from Rörer's notes of Luther's sermon on January 18, 1534 (WA 37:258–67).

is worth a hundred gulden,[7] or if a great prince and bishop himself baptized with great peal and pomp, just as they baptize their bells.[8] But since there is no such ornament or appearance, and God externally gives nothing more there than a handful of water, He must endure that it be scorned by the world. For, in brief, the world wants to have its eyes and ears filled, or it will think nothing of it.

It is, moreover, right for [God's Word and works] to be treated this way (so they think). "For," they say, "why would He act so unreasonably and not do things differently if He wants them to be given high honor and be regarded as a divine matter? If He is so great, mighty, judicious, and wise, He should undertake matters differently." But He does so for the precise purpose of making a fool out of the world's wisdom. Since it tries to split hairs and find fault with God's words and works, not allowing any of them to be right or good, He chooses to give it plenty of them and, despite everything, by such insignificant, despised words to accomplish things in His Christians which it can never understand or achieve. He is right to treat the world so, since it despises and refuses to hear or see such things because of their lowly appearance, so that as punishment for its stubborn malice the world robs itself of these lofty, good gifts of God and is led by the devil into all manner of error and abomination (even if under the great pretense of God's name).

We now see the Word and Sacraments suffering such things; we have been taught a lesson by our experience of the damage that has been done in Christendom, and must still expect such danger every day, especially since the shameful faction of the Anabaptists, by whom the devil intends to obscure and snuff out the true doctrine (after it has by God's grace been cleansed and made pure and is shining and giving off a little light), is already gaining ground everywhere. To combat this, then, we should honor, praise, and celebrate Baptism all the more, as much as we can, and make a greater effort to keep preaching about it. Therefore, let us discuss it once again, insofar as God grants us grace, as a correct lesson for the simple, so that people can know it correctly, make clear distinctions, and then pass sentence

---

[7] A gulden was the most valuable gold coin in common circulation. In 1529, the Torgau *Ordnung der Visitatoren* stipulated a senior pastor's annual salary as 80 gulden. A chaplain would receive 60 and a schoolmaster, 50 (Sehling, *Die Evangelischen Kirchenordnungen*, 1:679).

[8] The consecration of bells included many of the same ceremonies as used in Baptism. Amid psalms and prayers of consecration, a bell would be washed and anointed with oil, and incense would be placed under it. Once consecrated, the bell was considered a sacramental, having protective power against demons and storms. See S. Benz, "Glockenweihe," *LTK*[2] 4:966; Guido Fuchs, "Glockenweihe," *LTK*[3] 4:750–51. See also *Smalcald Articles* (1537) III XV 4 (Kolb-Wengert, p. 326; *Concordia*, p. 284); *Exhortation to All Clergy* (1530), AE 34:54.

on every sort of error that may rise against it. First, we will talk about what Baptism itself is in essence, then about its use and what it effects.

I.

We can break Baptism down into three distinct parts, which are water, Word, and God's command or order. Thus the water is not to be regarded as any other water, but that the Word (which is to say, God's Word) is in or with the water, and, third, God's will and power, or His command and institution, [is with it]. These are the three parts that are required for the complete essence and true definition of Baptism. They must be viewed in and with one another and not separated or divorced from one another, since together with one another they make true Baptism.

For it to be and be called a Sacrament, there first needs to be an outward, tangible sign or created thing by which God deals visibly with us, that we may be sure of it. It is not His will to work with us apart from outward means, solely by secret suggestions or special revelation from heaven.

But the outward work and sign does not by itself avail or do anything unless it is joined by His Word, by which the sign is made effective and we are made aware of what God is doing in us by this sign. Yet these must also be joined by a divine command by which we become certain of His will and work in this sign and Word.

It is necessary for me to show these three parts distinctly, since here once again there are three different kinds of teachers or masters, all of whom pervert and mutilate Baptism.

First, there are the crude cows and pigs who turn it into nothing but water and are unable to say more than: "Water is water and remains water." This person, whether he is a heathen, Turk, sectarian, or crude pope's ass,[9] is no better than a cow or pig, and what he says comes from a perfectly bestial understanding. For a cow knows nothing more than what it sees, that is, water; and whoever does not know God's Word will speak no differently from a horse or a mule (as Scripture calls them in Psalm 32 [:9]).

Such are today our despicable sect of Anabaptists, the devil's apostles, who run astray here and there in the land, preach against us, and from their great understanding grossly rebuke us and all Christians because we are such great fools who think we will be saved by water. They, of course, are most learned masters and wonderfully lofty spirits, who teach us this new, lofty trick that water is water. Who could have known or imagined this, if these most enlightened doctors had not come along? He might as well have

[9] This *Bapst-Esel* is described in the *Church Postil* (1540–44), sermon for Advent 2 on Luke 21:25–33, AE 75:99, paragraph 26.

asked a seven-year-old child about it, or gone to school awhile with oxen and cows, or have drunk with the pigs. Yet they are such buffoons and blockheads that they can spout nothing else against us but "water is water," and then assert their imaginary spirituality. I am surprised that, with all their emphasis on this and their shameful despising of water Baptism, they do not follow their own teaching and do away with it completely. They are still rebaptizing themselves and others, and then reproving themselves with their own deeds. If they do not let our Baptism stand (for which we have God's Word and command), then their baptism, which they regard as nothing but water, must count for far less.

This is the deception of the devil himself (who is nevertheless a crude buffoon of a devil). He makes monkeys and fools out of people with his deceptive outcry: "Do you not see that water is water? How can the same water that cows drink benefit souls and wash away sin?" This makes the insolent masses gape in astonishment, and at once they come out and say, "That's the truth for sure! Oh, how the devil deceived me so that I never saw or realized this!" Then they call it a precious and authentic doctrine and high art of the Spirit, if only it can say, "Water is water." Nevertheless, the poor are so easily deceived by this babbling, since [the masses] use many fine words and a loud noise to trump up their pronouncement that we teach that water (as water) washes the soul. They say, "Do not by any means believe that, for you see how they are misleading you into confiding and trusting in mere water, a created thing!"

These are desperate traitors and rogues indeed, who knowingly tear apart Baptism, sever and cut off the two best parts of it—namely, God's Word and command—and leave us with nothing but an empty shell or husk. They refuse to listen to or to look at our constant emphasis on these two parts (in and with the water), and then they brag against us with only one part, proclaiming this to be a special knowledge and Spirit. I, too (indeed, every peasant at his plow, without any knowledge), would be just as wise and learned if it were valid in one's own malice to sunder and tear apart what belongs together and is one essence. Who could not say, "How can Christ deliver me from sin, death, and the devil's power, if, as you yourself say, He is a man like any other man?" Likewise: "Why should I obey and submit to this man (such as my father, lord, or prince)? How is he different from me?" etc. But this may be described as the skill not of a Christian or of a godly man, but of a desperate rogue who wantonly tears apart what belongs to the whole person. For example, Christ is both true man and true God; father and mother or prince are not only common people like anyone else but also a person who has a special office by God's Word and command, from which he obtains, as it were, another nature and name, so that someone is not simply John or Nick but is called father or mother.

This crowd does the same thing with the most worthy Sacrament of Baptism when they regard only the water, as if God's Word and order were not present. To use a crude example, they act exactly as if you were to see the elector of Saxony walking in a black cloak after you had already seen the same cloak being beaten and dusted off in some tailor's shop, and accordingly you now decided, without another thought, to beat and slap it, and then said, "How is this cloth better than any other cloth?" Then you would certainly see what you had caused. They would promptly take you by the head[10] and beat your rags to a pulp in turn, and maybe in addition cut off your button,[11] as a malicious despiser of his royal person. It would not help for you to keep on saying, "I was not hitting the prince but the cloth." You would be met with the response: "It might be cloth like any other cloth, but do you not see that the prince is wearing it?" It is then no longer referred to as mere empty clothing or cloth, but both coat and man are together; indeed, it is a lordly, princely coat, since it is honored and worn by the prince himself.

I am obliged to present this in such a crude way so that it may be seen and grasped what scandalous spirits they are who separate and sever the Word from the water in such a way that Baptism is regarded as mere water; they so dishonor and slander it that it is awful to hear; they claim that they are doing God a great service by shamefully slandering and destroying it. But how will they endure when someday God says to them: "Tell Me, why did you slander My Baptism so abominably and call it a dog's bath when I Myself said that it should not be counted as mere water but as My (that is, God's) water? For My Word and command are in and with the water, for it is written: 'Go and baptize all nations in the name of the Father and of the Son and of the Holy Spirit,'" etc. [Matt. 28:19]. From this you ought to see what person this water has put on, and who is in it and with it—namely, the name of the Father, Son, and Holy Spirit—so that it is called the water of the divine Majesty. It must no longer be described as the kind of water that a cow drinks, for God clearly does not appoint His water (which contains His name and majesty) for the purpose of cows drinking it or pigs bathing in it, since it is not the creature or person that can be baptized and sanctified.[12]

---

[10] *kopff*

[11] *knöpfflin*. This seems to be Luther's play on words, in which "button" means as much as "head."

[12] Rörer's notes at this point read: "They have swallowed the Spirit. They did not say how the soul should be washed. Thus I say, beware, etc. Augsburg, Strassburg—you see how it is over for these altogether rich and mighty cities. Under the pope they did not teach this.

They are well aware of this, and yet maliciously and willfully dishonor and slander it, for which reason they will receive an all-the-more-unbearable judgment. As for us, we should watch out for them, learn this well, and make sure not to let the water and Word be thus severed and torn apart in holy Baptism and regarded simply as ordinary water. For if such a separation is made, we certainly know that that water is no Baptism (which it truly is not among them, where according to their doctrine they regard it as nothing but water and baptize without the Word and command). We, by contrast, say that, because it is united with God's Word, it neither can nor should be described as plain water any longer. Neither is it valid to say (as they do): "Water is water," since it is called Baptism not because it is water but because it has God's Word and command. These are the two main parts that set apart and distinguish this water from all other water and make a Baptism, or holy Sacrament, out of it, as we shall hear in more detail hereafter.

This is the first error regarding this Sacrament, made by those who regard only one part—namely, mere water—and separate and sever it from the best part so that, among them, it cannot but be a mere shell of doctrine. Next, there are others who are not so many (if God wills), nor are all of them as crude, though they still do not view Baptism properly. Nevertheless, they grant this much: that water and Word belong together, and there cannot be Baptism otherwise; they cite St. Augustine's statement: *Accedat verbum ad elementum, et fit Sacramentum.*[13] The water (or element) and Word together make a Sacrament. Yet there is still a weakness in that they omit the third part: God's command and order. Some think it sufficient to speak the words in the same way that a blessing is spoken over a created thing and suppose that by such speaking or by virtue of the same words something special is made of Baptism so that it becomes a Sacrament. These, too, are just crude teachers, as, indeed, the Papists are content to leave it at that and cannot see farther.[14]

Some, on the other hand, trying to be more subtle, even though they presuppose the two parts, still miss the third and even substitute something else for it. They see that simply taking water and speaking a word over it

---

Thus the Enthusiasts are having good luck. They find the people unprepared. The same could happen to you. One Enthusiast might snatch away in one hour what we have taught for twenty years. Surely it may come to pass" (WA 37:264.5–10). The "Enthusiasts" were those who insisted on the direct action of the Holy Spirit, not mediated by the external Word or Sacraments; see AE 60:332 n. 11.

[13] "When the Word comes to the element, it becomes a Sacrament" (Augustine, *Tractates on John* 80.3 [PL 35:1840; FC 90:117; NPNF[1] 7:344]).

[14] Rörer's notes at this point read: "Sectarian spirits who connect the Word and water together act like enchantresses who suppose that they make Baptism when they pronounce the words" (WA 37:262.27–30).

does not amount to a Baptism; so they say something else must be added to it, namely, faith. They try to base this on the words of Mark 16 [:16]: "Whoever believes and is baptized is saved," etc. Once again, then, they cite St. Augustine's statement (which is right after the previous one): *Non quia dicitur, sed quia creditur.*[15] The Sacrament is made out of water and Word, not because it is spoken, but because it is believed, etc. But this, too, is not said correctly. For they suppose (from improper understanding of this statement) that Word and water are a Sacrament as long as those who receive them have faith. Thus they base Baptism not on God's order but on men, as if the Word with the water is not efficacious for producing a Baptism until our faith is added to it; thus God's Word and work would first have to receive its power and effect from us.

This, too, is a wicked, harmful error (even though they are better than the first ones in this point, that they do not slander Baptism as mere water) which appeared long ago and has made deep inroads even today. For it is from this that the false argument about infant Baptism, which is so prevalent, first arose and stirred up rebaptism, and it is the strongest foundation used by this sect to substantiate its claim. They say: "You were baptized when you were still a child and did not believe. Therefore, your Baptism was nothing," etc. This is really the same as saying: "If you do not believe, God's Word and Sacrament are nothing. But if you believe, they are something. Therefore, only those who have faith receive true Baptism, whereas those who do not believe receive nothing but water and are not truly baptized. Therefore, we must baptize them anew, once they have begun to believe."

To this same error belong those who hold that Baptism administered by heretics or unbelievers is incorrect. Long ago, even excellent people (such as the holy martyr Cyprian) held this. There was a great deal of dispute over this, since much heresy and division arose in Christendom, and many were baptized by heretics. The question, then, was whether such Baptism was valid. These people (even St. Cyprian himself) fell so far [into error] that they regarded these Baptisms as wrong and said, "Whoever was baptized by a wicked, unbelieving minister (and especially by a heretic) must be baptized once again." To this end they falsely quoted and forced the words of Jesus Sirach (Ecclesiasticus 34 [:4]): *Ab inmundo quid mundabitur*, etc. "Whoever is himself unclean, how can he make anything clean? And whoever is a liar, how can he speak truth?" Likewise, Leviticus 15 [Num. 19:22]: "Whatever an unclean man touches becomes unclean." From this they try to conclude that, since the man who administered the Sacrament of Baptism was himself unclean and without faith, both the Baptism was unclean and the

[15] "Not because it is spoken, but because it is believed" (Augustine, *Tractates on John* 80.3 [PL 35:1840; FC 90:117; NPNF[1] 7:344]).

one who was baptized was not made clean by it. Thus it would not be a genuine Baptism, even though both water and Word were present together, since there was a lack of a person to administer the Baptism. Behold, this is getting personally involved in Baptism,[16] that is, basing and building it on men. Nevertheless, it has made great inroads by its great, noble appearance and, as was said, has cast down great men and attracted the masses.

To counteract this error, one should learn to recognize and view Baptism correctly and completely from God's Word. For it all comes from disregarding and severing the third part which belongs to Baptism (and which should probably be called the first), that is, God's order and command. It is by this that He has reserved Baptism completely for Himself and permits neither you nor anyone to add something to it in order for it to be a Baptism. I may be the one baptizing, and you the one baptized, but it is not therefore mine or yours, but Christ's Baptism. In short, everyone can give and receive it if it has already been made and instituted, but no one should or can make or institute it except Him alone.

Just listen to His words: "Go and baptize all nations in the name of the Father and of the Son and of the Holy Spirit" [Matt. 28:19]. "Whoever believes and is baptized is saved," etc. [Mark 16:16]. These are not the words which we speak over the Baptism, but the words of command which institute Baptism. For it is not the priest or minister but He who makes Baptism who says, "Go and baptize," that is, "Here you have My command and order. This is My will and bidding: that you baptize in the name of the Father, Son, and Holy Spirit. If anyone receives the Word and water together, it is a Baptism; if anyone believes in addition, he will be saved thereby." Here there is something beyond the two parts of Word and water; otherwise it would be far from sufficient to dip in water and speak the words "I baptize you," etc.—even if faith were present—without having a clear, certain command to do so.

Above all, it is necessary to know whence Baptism comes, or by what means it is a Baptism, so that it is possible to answer the question "Who told you to put water and Word together?" or "From what source and by what means are you certain that this is a holy Sacrament?" If the two parts were enough, I and everyone could make a Baptism whenever we chose—indeed, as many sacraments as we wished. For then I myself could take something created by God (whatever I wanted) and speak God's Word over it, just as the Papists do with their holy water, salt, fire, chrism,[17] candles, spices, wafers, altars, and consecration of churches; they say: "I bless" or "I consecrate you, O salt, spice, wax, chasuble, altar, cowl, etc., in the name of the Father, Son,

[16] *die Tauffe zu sich selbs gezogen*, literally, "drawing Baptism to oneself."

[17] I.e., oil for anointing.

and Holy Spirit," and then read psalms and other prayers over it. Since God's Word and God's creature are together here, one could conceivably say from St. Augustine: *Accedit verbum ad elementum, et fit sacramentum.*[18]

Why is this not so valid and efficacious as Baptism? Why do we not make a sacrament out of holy water and salt, all monks' and nuns' cowls, and the candles of Saints Blaise and Agatha[19]—indeed, from every manner of blessing and incantation?[20] When the foul enchantresses and witches blow in a cow's ear and speak the names of God and the saints, both the created thing, or element, and God's Word come together. Why, then, is this not a sacrament, too, since you say that the two parts of Word and element produce a Sacrament?

Answer: Yes, it is true; it takes those two parts. But they themselves are still not enough to make a Sacrament. That takes one more thing: having the Trinity on our side, which is to say, a divine order and command. If you can add in the fact that the divine Majesty in heaven says, "I have ordered and commanded it," those two parts conclude and make valid what is called a Sacrament. Otherwise (as I have said) anything a man might imagine could be a Sacrament. There is no one too simple to take God's Word into his mouth, apply it to a created thing, and make something with it. That is the stuff of sorcerers and devil's whores[21] who steal milk[22] or switch infants in the cradle. They use no bad words, but strictly good, holy words and names, and in addition to that have something created by God. This is what happens, and the devil does his best to help, for he delights in inspiring such foolishness under God's name and thereby deceiving people into thinking that it is an entirely godly affair, since they speak only good words.[23]

Here, however, it is right to be concerned with regard to this third part, whether God has commanded and ordered you[, for example,] to grasp the

---

[18] See above, p. 20 n. 13.

[19] On February 3, the feast day of St. Blaise (d. 316), bishop of Sebaste and martyr, those with throat pain were supposed to be able to find remedy as the priest held two lit candles crosswise at the throat. See M. J. Costelloe, "Blaise of Sebaste, St.," in *New Catholic Encyclopedia*, 2nd ed. (Detroit: Thomson Gale, 2003), 2:428. On "St. Agatha's lights," see *Exhortation to All Clergy* (1530), AE 34:58.

[20] See *Exhortation to All Clergy* (1530), AE 34:55–58, for Luther's list of such invented sacraments.

[21] *Teufelshuren*, i.e., witches. For Luther's views of witchcraft, see AE 76:72–73 n. 10.

[22] Witches were believed to dry up the milk supply of nursing mothers, thus causing infant death; see Lyndal Roper, *Witch Craze: Terror and Fantasy in Baroque Germany* (New Haven: Yale University Press, 2004), p. 119.

[23] Rörer's notes at this point add: "as if he would say, 'I use no bad words, but the best words.' But say, 'An element or creature and Word of God are required for the Sacrament, but so is a third [part], that God commanded you [to do] it' " (WA 37:261.30–31).

handle of a hatchet or an ax or a maniple[24] in order to make a cow give milk. Has He commanded you to consecrate and bless palms and spices and use them to accomplish what you wish?[25] If you can say that He has commanded you to do that, then we will regard it is as a work of God. But when you decide to do this using your own judgment and at the same time say, "I am using a good thing that God has created, and God's true, holy Word and name"—that does not hold at all. This is not obedience to God's command but to your own presumption—indeed, flagrant disobedience—and work and service of the devil.

It would be something if you could show God's commandment or instruction and say: "I did not come up with this or choose this on my own or undertake it based on my own idea. Rather, God told me to take this created thing and Word and use it in this way," etc. We can do this here with Baptism by showing how He gives us the command and tells us to baptize, that is, to dip the person in the water and at the same time to speak the words ("in the name of the Father, Son, and Holy Spirit"). Neither I nor any man personally decided on such baptizing with water (as do sorcerers or the Papistic wafer-consecrators);[26] I have not invented the words nor spoken them out of my own imagining, but both water and Word are clearly and plainly identified for me, contained in His command, and thereby preserved.

In nothing (however insignificant it is) does He desire anything to be done by us out of our own choosing or imagining—or whatever people want to call it—or to be dealt with apart from His Word and sure, clear command. Much less will He tolerate such things in these high matters, which are properly God's works, in which we have no place to act or do anything. For this reason He includes and encloses them in His command. So that we may be sure of this, He guards them so closely that He Himself specifically identifies all the parts, clearly expresses what signs or created things He wants, and personally provides the form of the words and how they should go. We must use these exact signs and none other, and these very words and none other.

So just as it is invalid for sorceresses to use something created by God along with God's Word—since the third part, God's personal command to use both created object and Word, is not present—neither is it at all valid

[24] *handzwehl*, i.e., a vestment worn at Mass, consisting of a silk cloth worn on the left arm near the wrist.

[25] On the misuse of palm branches in popular piety, see *Exhortation to All Clergy* (1530), AE 34:56. On the blessing and use of spices and other items, see *Smalcald Articles* (1537) III XV 5 (Kolb-Wengert, p. 326; *Concordia*, p. 284).

[26] *Fladenweiher*, a pejorative term for Roman Catholic priests, perhaps due to their attention to the consecration of the bread and wine of the Mass as the most important part of their ministry, as opposed to the ministry of preaching the Word of God and distributing the Sacraments to the people.

here for it to be a Sacrament or true Baptism without or outside, or beside and beyond, God's clear command. For instance, if you baptized a child with water and spoke over it an Our Father or something else from Scripture and God's Word, it would not be called a true Baptism. Neither is it enough for you to say, "Well, the water required for Baptism and God's Word are both present!" For the third part is still missing, because God did not tell you to speak those words.

Likewise, if you decided to use something besides the created object mentioned and specified for it, and yet spoke the proper words ("I baptize you in the name of the Father, Son, and Holy Spirit"), that, too, would not be baptizing, but jesting and making a mockery of the Sacrament, since it willfully bypasses the order and command (which plainly identifies the created object). It is the same in the Sacrament of Christ's body and blood: if the command and institution are not kept, it is not a Sacrament. For instance, if a man reads the Ten Commandments, the Creed, or some verse or psalm over the bread and wine on the altar; or again takes something else such as gold, silver, meat, oil, or water instead of bread and wine (even though he uses the right words of Christ's institution)—that would clearly not be Christ's body and blood. Even though God's Word and something created by God are present, it still is not a Sacrament, for His order and command, in which He referred to bread and wine and spoke the words "Take, eat; this is My body," etc., "Drink; this is My blood," etc., are not present. In short, you are not to make a choice or determination on your own about either Word or object, nor of your own accord to include or leave out any action whatsoever. Rather, His command and order should determine for you both Word and object, which you are to leave completely intact.

In this way, learn to take the three parts together, for therein you have all that Baptism is in itself and in its natural essence. Then you are able to form and provide a proper, complete definition when someone asks: "Tell me, what is Baptism?" Namely: "Baptism is both water and God's Word, ordained and given by His command."[27] For He commanded us to take the created thing (namely, water) and speak the words in His name. Thus when both of these things are done at His command, it is called a true Baptism, and without doubt is one. Thus these three parts always remain together, and none is without the other; they are linked together like a chain—indeed, united together like parts of a body.

Similarly, in the other holy Sacrament of Christ's body and blood, it says that our Lord Jesus Christ took both the bread and the cup, blessed them, gave them to His disciples, and said, "Take and eat"; likewise: "Drink of it, all [of you]," etc. [Matt. 26:26–27]. Here, too, there is one part called an element

[27] Cf. *Small Catechism* (1529) IV 1–2 (Kolb-Wengert, p. 359; *Concordia*, p. 339).

or created thing that is visible and tangible, namely, bread and wine. Next, there is also the Word, in His saying: "This is My body, which is given for you. This is My blood, which is shed for you" [cf. Luke 22:19–20]. Yet these two parts would still not give us the Sacrament by which we would be able to eat and drink Christ's body and blood. For that, another part is required, and He makes it plain when He says, "This do," etc. [Luke 22:19]. That is: "I bid, command, and order, and hereby desire it to be commanded and ordered, that you do these things (as often as you will do them), namely, take bread and wine and at the same time speak these My words, and so eat My body and blood." This part binds the other two together and assures us that we have the true Sacrament.

With this instruction and understanding, then, you yourself can proceed and become an expert skilled enough to judge rightly and with certainty and at the same time to give the right answer with ease and to refute all sorts of false doctrine and nonsense from the sectarian spirits opposed to Baptism. For example, the first ones who slandered it became excited about the first part, and with loud crying and lavish words sounded forth: "How is a handful of water (being a created thing) supposed to benefit the soul or blot out sin? The Spirit has to do it. Just think and consider yourself: the soul is not truly a physical thing that can be washed or cleansed with water. So you see, they deceive and mislead you into trusting not in God but in a created thing." Then they go and sputter on and on about the spiritual washing of the soul, etc. By such words they attract the unwitting masses to themselves so that they think that this is how it is, and cannot be turned from it. Yet fundamentally it is nothing else than false and fictitious deception and babbling with which they slanderously and treacherously defame our dear Baptism by knowingly and maliciously stripping away the best part and thrusting it from sight, and then sputter about mere water.

You are therefore perfectly right to counter such people by saying: "You shameless spirit of lies! You yourself are well aware that we do not teach Baptism as plain water. Rather, you use this pretense simply to slander the most worthy, holy Sacrament, and thereby lead poor souls astray. We have (God be praised!) enough eyes, senses, and reason—indeed, enough faculty of taste and touch—to see and understand what water is, and are equally capable of saying, 'Water is water' (which is your highest skill). But you preach Baptism as though it were nothing more than water and strip it of the most important parts (God's Word and command, by which that water is sanctified and becomes a Sacrament), as though they were nothing or did not count. The devil, your master and the father of lies [John 8:44], has bidden you to do so; and so you act as a criminal and evildoer, corruptor and slanderer of God's majesty, Word, and works, and deceive the people with false words so that they see no more in it than a cow sees.

"For you must confess (no thanks to you or the devil) that Christ Himself instituted this Baptism and added to it His Word or command, bidding us to baptize in the name of the Father, Son, and Holy Spirit, and at the same time promising: 'Whoever is thus baptized and believes will be saved,' etc. [Mark 16:16]. You must not set this out of our sight and snatch it away, as though it counted for nothing and did nothing, and meanwhile point us to an imaginary realm and promulgate a spirituality dreamed up by yourself." For we know and also teach (God be praised!), more and better than they do, what the Holy Spirit works in us, but we will not let them pry us away from this Baptism and Sacrament and point us instead to an empty corner, where they gape after the Spirit and seek private revelation outside of the Word and God's order. For we know that it is precisely through the Word and Sacrament and through no other means that He wills to work with us.

Thus we do not need to look elsewhere for the Spirit if we have this Sacrament of Baptism, since we hear from Christ's words and institution that the name of the Holy Spirit is present along with that of the Father and Son (that is, of the whole divine Majesty). And since God's name and Word are in it, you are not permitted to regard it as plain and simple water that does no more than bathwater, but rather as the kind of water by which we are cleansed from sin and, as Scripture calls it, a washing of regeneration [Titus 3:5] by which we are reborn into eternal life, about which we will hear more hereafter.

These words should suffice to answer those who regard Baptism strictly as a washing of the body and pay no heed to the Word or God's command. So, too, you can use the very same ideas to answer those others who, while speaking well of Baptism, nevertheless view it wrongly with regard to its third part and do not establish and base it on God's command and order, but, like any human work, on our faith and worthiness; they act as if it were not enough that God ordained and commanded it to be thus, but that it first had to be confirmed by us and was invalid without the addition of our faith.

Against this we say that, whatever the condition of my faith, whether or not it comes or stays, does not add to or take away anything at all from Baptism. Even if I never have faith, Baptism is still true and complete, for it does not depend on my faith or lack of faith but on His order and institution. If a crafty Jew came along to deceive us, pretended that he wanted to become a Christian, and requested Baptism; if the pastor or priest dipped him in the water before our eyes and said the words "I baptize you in the name and at the command of God and of the Lord Jesus Christ," etc.—he would truly and genuinely be baptized, even if he completely discounted it in his heart and afterward mocked and slandered it in public. For if God ordained and commanded it, what does He care whether you do not believe? Would that mean that His order and command were nothing or were hampered by your unbelief and misuse? It would remain true, as St. Paul says in Romans 3 [:4]: even if all men were false and liars, yet His Word and order remain true and unmoved.[28] If you believe it and use it rightly, you are blessed. If you do not believe, you receive it to your damnation.

For we can use Baptism (like the other Sacrament and order of God) for harm and ruin, so that by the same kind of Baptism one man is saved and another damned. But this does not belong to the essence (which we are discussing now) but to the power and use of Baptism. It is a very different thing to talk about what Baptism is in itself, for this requires no human doing, but strictly an element or created thing and God's Word, both instituted by Him and contained in His command. As said before, He has reserved it for Himself, so that no man has anything to do in it or add to it; it rests on Him alone as our sure foundation and cannot fail or deceive us, as men fail and deceive. Therefore, when this (namely, God's command) is present beside the two parts, it is certainly a true, complete Sacrament, even if it is not received rightly or used so that it attains to its power and efficacy.

It is the same way with God's other ordinances in physical, created things. For example, the sun rises in the sky each day and runs its course and is always the same sun, shining and giving light as it was created and commanded to do (Genesis 1 [:14–18]) without being moved or hindered; it does this even if a man does not see or perceive it, because he is blind or has closed the windows and everything so that it does not shine on him or give him warmth. In short, all God's creations proceed and abide in their essence and work as they have been ordered, even if they do not do this and carry it out for everyone. In the same way, the holy Sacraments (insofar as they are treated and administered according to God's command) are authentic, complete according to their essence, and salutary works of God. The fact that they do not benefit all people, however, is to be blamed not on the Sacrament but on the one who does not use it rightly and is not receptive to its power.

Now, since we have this doctrine and trustworthy account, we should learn to extol and speak well of this most worthy Sacrament over against those spirits who despise and slander it. For from what has been said already, every man can certainly realize that Baptism with water must not be scorned as a worthless human invention, but rather given high regard and honor as

---

[28] Rörer's notes at this point read: "Even if it were true that a child did not have faith, and even today is baptized in unbelief, it is not an incorrect Baptism on account of the sin of the man. Christ does not say, 'He who believes and confesses will be [saved].' He commands it of each person in his faith" (WA 37:281.11–14).

a holy Sacrament and special work of the divine Majesty; it is fitting to call it a holy, heavenly—indeed, divine—water.

I am not saying all this with regard to the great things which the power and benefit of Baptism effect and accomplish, which will be discussed after this, but with regard to the way its natural essence is in itself. Here I am saying that, if you look at how this water is bound up with God's Word and name, inasmuch as He Himself commands the words "in the name of the Father and Son and Holy Spirit" (as if to say, "I, God the Father, I, God the Son, and [I, God] the Holy Spirit, sanctify this water") to be spoken over it, then you cannot say that it is merely aqueous or terrestrial water, or (as the sects call it) "bathwater" and a "dogbath." Rather, you must say that it is a water of the divine Majesty Himself and that by it not we men but God Himself (by our hands) does the baptizing and has infused and woven His name into it so that it is blended together with it and may even be referred to as "God-filled water."

For example, when you touch a piece of iron that is lying in the forge and glowing, you touch not mere iron but fire which burns. Even if you see no fire but only iron (just as it is not seen to glow by day as much as by night), it is nevertheless not only iron but both iron and fire. In fact, it is so permeated by fire that nothing is felt or detected but pure fire.[29] In the same way, Baptism should be viewed as incorporated into God's name and completely permeated by it so that it is one essence, and thus has become a thing far different from other water. It is like an excellent tonic prepared for a sick man, which, even though made from water, has so much precious spice and sugar dissolved into it that no water can be tasted in it any longer. Yet here is a far more excellent water sweetened with God's name; in fact, it is thoroughly divine, though to the eye nothing is visible but water.

We must not think it an insignificant matter when God's name is present. For that is the only thing that cleanses and sanctifies all things and makes and does all things. In summary, God's name is nothing else than the almighty power of God and eternal purity, holiness, and life. Wherever it is used by God's command, it cannot be without fruit and benefit, but must do great, indescribable things and act in accordance with His nature. Thus in Baptism, too, it cannot but produce clean and holy and utterly heavenly, godly men, as we shall see in greater detail hereafter.

Now, since this is certain and indisputable, it must also follow that Baptism is something truly spiritual; indeed, it must contain and carry with it nothing but the Spirit, and is not the nonsense of the sectarian spirits with which they turn people from the Word and all the way cry with hostility:

[29] Luther often uses this same illustration: see, e.g., *Adoration of the Sacrament* (1523), AE 36:282.

"The Spirit must do it; external things (such as water) cannot benefit the soul," etc. Yet they are never able themselves to teach with certainty what the Spirit or something spiritual is, or how and by what means they are arrived at. Instead, they point people to some empty corner where they themselves dream up a spirit.

Here we say: "If you wish to teach me what the Spirit is and where to find Him, you must not point me to an imaginary realm, but only look to God's Word. If you have this, you have no need to engage in many disputes or to keep gaping and searching. You will never find Him outside of it, even if you look your whole life and dream and think yourself to death. Rather, you must look for Him here, where He has set Himself by the Word, inasmuch as He institutes Baptism in His own name. Or do you dare to say that the name of the divine Majesty is something else than pure Spirit? The name or person of the Holy Spirit is clearly expressed in it! Therefore, He must certainly be present there. Since He is there, the water, too, must be spiritual, and He must be at work in it and by it give the Spirit or make spiritual men. Thus Baptism can truly be called spiritual water, both in itself—or in its essence—and in its work in those by whom it is received in faith.

Behold, when Baptism is viewed this way and laid out accordingly, it becomes something greater and more glorious than can ever be sufficiently expressed or comprehended—indeed, more glorious than heaven and earth combined. For the divine Majesty is present there and performing His highest work in it (namely, giving us Himself and making us completely newborn and saving us, as you shall hear), all by putting His name there. He has commanded that His name not be used in vain but kept sacred and holy above all things [Exod. 20:7], since by it we have God Himself and all that pertains to our salvation and eternal life; it accomplishes everything in heaven and earth. Therefore, I should not let Baptism be despised and slandered, but raise it as high and honor it as much as I am obliged to honor the name and majesty of God. I should not tolerate the blind, erring spirits who do not know what the Spirit is or where He is, and yet shout on and on about it and blaspheme against the true Spirit.

But if you say: "Why do you make much only of Baptism with water and not of other created things, since you yourself say that wherever God's name and Word is, the Spirit is too? Does it not follow, then, that wherever God's name or Word are added to a created thing, the Spirit must be there, too, and thus everyone must be able to produce or find the Spirit everywhere?" Answer: This requires the third part, which I discussed above: God's command and order. It is not enough for you to choose any created thing (even though all created things are good) and to use God's name along with it. Rather, it requires the command or the sort of word that tells you to add the name of God to this created thing. This does not give you the freedom to use God's name and created things however you wish. He commanded you not to use His name in vain [Exod. 20:7]. By this He acknowledges that the name, which (in itself) is full of Spirit and every good, can nevertheless be misused apart from and contrary to the Spirit.

Misusing it is defined as not using it as He bids and commands, but barging in without Him and trying to act as we ourselves conceive, as sorcerers and devil's whores[30] do. Likewise, false teachers and sects use His name and Word for sin and shame, even though it is the true, holy name, and the name and Word of the very same true Spirit of God who is in Baptism. This is enough discussion of the first part, concerning what Baptism is in itself.

II.

Here let us examine why the most worthy Sacrament of Baptism was instituted, and what purpose it should serve or what it should accomplish (though this already has been touched on above somewhat): God ordained and commanded His Word and Baptism to be administered in order that people might be saved (that is, delivered from sin and death and brought into God's kingdom and eternal life). For the text reads: "*Whoever believes and is baptized* will be saved," etc. [Mark 16:16].

Here you have the reason why, the end to which it is called Baptism, and what its ultimate meaning is: to be a washing for the soul or (as St. Paul calls it [Titus 3:5]) "a washing of new birth," by which we are born out of this fleshly, sinful birth and way of life to the new, spiritual life, in which we are justified before God and become heirs of heaven. Thus it is not to be taken as an empty sign or a fruitless, useless baptizing or bath, as it was long ago in the Old Testament. Then the priests, adorned with their beautiful finery of gold and silk, offered their sacrifices and had various washings and purifications, which were merely signs and nevertheless great burdens which were good for nothing except that the priests were allowed to eat and drink of what they served in the temple. For others, however, it was nothing but a duty and weight imposed on them as a sign that they were God's people, just as the father of a family daily imposes on his servant this or that task (so that he recognizes and regards him as his master) and gives him bread and payment in return.

Here, however, it is something completely different. For through this Baptism, that external washing and baptizing is all abolished and no longer imposed on us or demanded from us as a law or work for us to do. Rather, it is only ordained for the purpose of serving and giving to us not something

[30] *Teufelshuren*, i.e., witches.

physical and transitory, but eternal grace, purity or holiness, and eternal life. It is fittingly called "a washing of new birth" and "the true washing of rejuvenation,"[31] since whoever washes in it is rejuvenated and reborn, not from his mother's womb as before, which is the old birth, but from sin to righteousness, from guilt and condemnation to innocence and grace, and from death into eternal life.

To go into more detail and to show where and by what means Baptism derives such power, what high and glorious honor it is given by God Himself, and how much effort He has put into it, let us go on and relate the text and events of the Baptism of our Lord Christ referred to by all the evangelists, but especially as described by St. Matthew 3 [:13–17], which reads:

> At that time, Jesus came from Galilee to the Jordan to John, that He might be baptized by him. But John prevented Him and said, "I have need to be baptized by You, and do You come to me?" But Jesus answered and said, "For now let it be so. Thus it is fitting for us to fulfill all righteousness." Then he permitted Him.
>
> And when Jesus was baptized, He went up at once out of the water. And behold, heaven opened above Him. And John saw the Spirit of God like a dove descend and come upon Him. And behold, a voice spoke from heaven: "This is My dear Son in whom I am well pleased."

This is the text that teaches us how to praise and esteem Baptism correctly. It is a glorious revelation the likes of which were never heard or seen before and cannot be expressed in words. However, this text is read by both the sects and all those who are under the pope, and the revelation and beautiful portrait stands open and clear before the eyes of all men. If only all who go by the name "Christian," however wise or pious they be, would not neglect this, but would open their eyes and look for a moment at what happened here, and what it must mean, since God personally revealed Himself here in visible form from heaven and allowed Himself to be heard with a physical voice! How far and wide all the world would run and hasten after it, if we had never heard of it before, and then found out that there were a place on the edge of the world where a glorious revelation such as this had been heard! But the fact is, the world will be blind and not regard such things even if they appear before its eyes and ears, since they do not have so great and noble an appearance as the world might wish, but are reported without a flourish, in plain, simple words. Meanwhile, as a reward for its scorn, the world must fasten its lips and eyes on other things that it has thought or

---

[31] *Jüngel Bad*, an expression apparently coined by Luther. Luther was fond of the comparison between the fountain of youth and Baptism: see *Die kleine Antwort auf Herzog Georgs nächstes Buch* (1533), WA 38:150; sermon of October 12, 1537, WA 45:172f.; *Sermons on John 1–2* (1537–38), AE 22:174; *[Second] Sermon at the Baptism of Bernhard von Anhalt* (1540), AE 51:328; sermon of January 10, 1546, AE 58:394.

dreamed up itself. But let us at least open our heart a little and have regard for this appearance or revelation and esteem it as highly as we can, for it is so great and high that we will never reach the top of it.[32]

First, we see how the Lord Christ Himself honors Baptism here by coming from the land of Galilee to John the Baptist at the Jordan, right when He was about to begin and enter into His office for which He was sent, that He Himself might go around and preach. Yet it is His will not to enter into it before He Himself has first been baptized by John. Now John (with both his preaching and Baptism) was present only in order to point to the coming Christ, and would not continue or apply beyond that, but would hand everything over to Christ at whatever time He should come. Thus he was nothing more than Christ's minister, to admonish the people to amend their ways and to receive the coming Christ as the true Lord and Savior who would personally baptize them, that is, cleanse and purify them from sin and justify them. Yet Christ comes right when He was to begin and John's office and Baptism were to cease, and wills to be baptized by His minister first.

Why does He do this? Or for what purpose does He need Baptism? Being Himself the man to whom John points the people, He has no need of it in order to be cleansed and purified by it. It appears, moreover, to be of no use at all for Him, since John himself says that it is a Baptism for repentance [Matt. 3:11], and He, being born free from sin by the Holy Spirit of the Virgin, and having nothing but holiness in all His body and life, was pure and holy already and was the very one by whom all people must be made holy. Thus it was fitting for St. John and his baptizing to cease with this Man. He refuses to baptize Him, confesses that he must be baptized by Him, renounces and retires from his office and from baptizing, and makes room for Christ.

It is good, then, to conclude that Christ did this not for His own sake but for our sake. As stated, He personally had no need at all of Baptism or of the office of preaching, but did it all that by it we might be saved. This is why He honors this office so highly that He not only ordains Baptism and commands it to be administered (which would be enough) but also receives it Himself from His minister, that He might confirm it and by His action and example teach that Baptism should be held in high regard and given glorious praise.

For by doing this, He Himself shows that Baptism must be a blessed affair, abounding in grace, since He not only provides His Word and office for it but also sinks and puts Himself into it and touches this water with

[32] The following section is adapted mainly from Rörer's notes of Luther's sermon on February 1, 1534 (WA 37:270–75).

His own holy body; indeed, He sanctifies it and fills it with blessing.[33] Just observe what sort of person He is: the Son both of God the Father from eternity and of the Virgin; true, almighty God and Lord of all creation, and true man, except without any sin, full of righteousness and holiness, so that He sanctifies all things through Himself.

What people, then, would dare disparage Baptism with water (which this almighty person and His holy body has touched) as no better than the water that a cow drinks? Indeed, how can a man be so callous as to feel no shame in his heart nor the need to lift up his eyes when he sees the high person of Christ (to the honor of Baptism and for our good) Himself come to John, desire Baptism, and refuse to step up and preach without being baptized, which He would certainly have the right and power to do? A sin-ridden sack of maggots[34] has the audacity not only to disparage Baptism but even to vilify it with such blasphemous terms ("dogbath" and "bathwater"), which are frightening for a Christian to hear! They must be an accursed lot in the pit of hell, knowingly and brazenly to say such slanderous things against holy Baptism that, in return for their diabolical wickedness, God so confounds and blinds them that they have no eyes or ears to see or hear how Christ Himself honors and sanctifies Baptism. Even a simpleton would be able to notice and conclude that, since the man Jesus Christ, the Son of God (who has no need to be baptized or sanctified by the water, but Himself sanctifies the water), nevertheless refuses to remain unbaptized without it, He esteems and thinks much of it and wants us to do the same. Even if it did not effect or give anything (which however is impossible), and even if He had not commanded the whole world to be baptized, nevertheless Christ's example is enough [to show] that Baptism should be honored and eagerly received.

In the second place, holy Baptism is given even more honor and praise here by a great and glorious sign and wonder from heaven. As though it were not enough that Christ Himself submitted to Baptism from His minister John, as soon as He comes out of the water, the whole heaven opens up so that the divine Majesty comes down and appears visibly. Although it is told simply, it is certainly the greatest sign and most glorious revelation ever heard or seen. Here God actually shows Himself, not as He did to the fathers by private revelation, nor in a form not His own[35] through an angel, but personally and in His own majesty and publicly across the entire heavens, where there is no darkness or cloud, but only light and gleaming brightness; and not by mere visions and mute signs, but with a living voice and glorious

---

[33] Rörer's notes here add: "Happy water, that touched this body and person!" (WA 37:271.17).

[34] *maden sack*. This was one of Luther's favorite colorful expressions for human mortality.

[35] *jnn frembder gestalt*, or "in a foreign [or alien] form."

proclamation. All three persons of the Godhead, distinct and through three different forms or images—thus the Majesty itself—was completely poured out and displayed over the Baptism of Christ.

In this way, the mouths of the pernicious spirits who disparage Baptism were shut. For how would or could a man praise it more highly than we see it honored and praised here by the divine Majesty with this exceedingly glorious revelation? Heaven, which was shut before, opens and becomes nothing but light—indeed, nothing but doors and windows—and the entire Trinity presides over the Baptism and sanctifies it by His presence, and at the same time bears witness to it and preaches at it, as we shall hear in greater detail.

Of course, this image and revelation did not occur for the sake of the Lord Christ any more than He received Baptism for His own sake. Why would He need the Father (along with the Holy Spirit) to reveal Himself to Him and preach about Him, since He was always personally with and in Christ? This all happened for our sake who were to believe in Him, be baptized in His name, and be saved, as an eternal image of Christendom, in which God has shown Himself publicly, made Himself both seen and heard, and drawn so near to us that He could not be nearer. It was, moreover, done in the most pleasant and tender manner and by the most comforting proclamation (as we shall hear). With Him surely was the countless multitude of all the heavenly host, standing there before their Lord and Maker to the glory of Baptism. This all happened so that we might learn what He wishes to do by Baptism and what we receive in it.

Just as this glorious splendor of the divine Majesty was visibly present there once, the same thing still happens in a spiritual and invisible manner for everyone who is baptized into Christ. This scene depicts the eternal pattern (as stated), that the divine Majesty Himself will always be present at Baptism. Moreover, to assure us of this, Christ Himself plainly expresses as much at the institution of Baptism when He tells us to baptize "in the name of the Father, of the Son, and of the Holy Spirit" [Matt. 28:19]. Thus the words harmonize perfectly with this scene and present and display the very same faith that this picture displays visibly to our eyes, lest we have any doubt that, where Baptism is, there heaven is certainly open and the entire Trinity present, sanctifying and blessing through Himself the one being baptized.

Again, contrary to those who slander Baptism, you can prove from this, first, that it is not the plain, simple water which a cow drinks, but a water that is blessed and hallowed by the divine Majesty and (as stated above) completely permeated with God.[36] We clearly see all the persons being named at

---

[36] *gantz durchGottet*, or "filled with God." This expression apparently was coined by Luther. See above, p. 29.

the institution of Baptism and shown and depicted as actually present in this account. Even though we no longer see before our eyes the Holy Spirit hovering physically over Christ in the form of a dove, nor hear the Father's voice, nevertheless this picture remains in our hearts constantly. For it was presented on that occasion for our sake, as a sign and testimony along with the words, in which we hear and believe the very same thing that St. John saw there. Just as it is said there *in praesenti visione* ["in the vision that is present"],[37] so it is said here *in nomine Patris et Filii et Spiritus sancti* ["in the name of the Father and of the Son and of the Holy Spirit," Matt. 28:19]. There He shows Himself in visible form; here, in His Word and name.[38]

Second, this picture must not be construed as useless and powerless, like the picture or portrait of a man, sketched out on a panel or in a mirror, where there is nothing but paint brushed on or a reflection—an illusion which has and possesses nothing more. It is, rather, nothing less than a living thing by which the divine Majesty depicts and portrays Himself, and thus is also truly and personally present, in such a way that it is not a mere picture but the essence itself—indeed, nothing but Life and Power. He does not come down in order simply to produce a mere vision, like a shadow or phantom (as an illusionist does), but to accomplish His work and display His power there. This is not the work that He works and performs generally with creation in creating and sustaining it, or accomplishing something through it, but the proper, true, and highest work of the divine Majesty, which concerns our redemption and eternal salvation and which belongs to each person of the divine Majesty: the Father is in it with His light and majesty, the Son with His blood, and the Holy Spirit with His fire. Therefore, this water or Baptism must not be viewed as a mere washing with water or a bare symbol, for wherever God binds Himself to being present, He must also be powerful and accomplish great, divine things. Why else would He show Himself visibly and use such splendor and extraordinary means?

All these things, then, took place so that in this picture we might grasp what God has in mind here and what His will and intention is with Baptism (which things He will also display and interpret afterward with His proclamation), namely, that He wills therein to give us His majesty, light, and power, and Himself with all His possessions and powers. What are His powers? The power to take away death, sin, and all our calamity and to give us eternal righteousness, life, and joy instead. How does He do that? By the blood of His beloved Son, which is the price that was paid, by which we were secured the ability to find favor with Him. As Christ says, "God so loved the world that He gave His only Son," etc. [John 3:16].

---

[37] Rörer's notes here read: "in the presence of the Father, Son, Holy Spirit" (WA 37:272.13–14).

[38] Rörer's notes here add: "invisibly" (WA 37:272.14).

But for us to sense and feel these things by faith, the Holy Spirit must enlighten and kindle us with His fire. Since this all takes place in this holy Sacrament of Baptism, it is not fitting to see it as a cow sees it—as being water and being wet—but as the blood of the Son of God and as the fire of the Holy Spirit. Herein the Son sanctifies through His blood, the Holy Spirit cleanses with His fire, the Father enlivens[39] by His light and radiance, so that all three are personally present and simultaneously performing the same divine work and pouring all their power into Baptism.

Who will express this inexpressible grace and glory, that God should reveal Himself this way and want to be our own and to give us all things? Or what man would dare despise Baptism after seeing and hearing how God Himself ordained it, instituted it, and honors and graces it with His presence, indeed, baptizes with His own fingers—provided it follows and is kept according to His command and order (apart from an enchantress or sectarian spirit interfering with it)? For He bids and says, "Go and baptize in My name." In other words: "You shall act and behave precisely as though I Myself were baptizing, along with the Father and the Holy Spirit." What more glorious and greater things could be said or thought about Baptism? Heaven and earth are too small to contain them.[40]

Third, and greatest of all, is the fact that here God the Father Himself speaks and delivers a sermon on the Baptism of the Lord Christ. All the world, and whoever is able to run, should run to hear that preacher who is God the Father speaking from heaven. If we knew of a place where God Himself could be heard to speak, even if it were at the world's end, we might wish to do just that. How blessed we would call those who experienced it! Yet there it lies before our eyes. Not only did He speak once in those days, so that only those people were able to praise it, but He does us the favor of having it preached perpetually to all who came after them and are still to come until the Last Day, so that we are able to hear it daily, if only we were so godly as to open our ears and our heart and try to understand it.

So let us hear how the Father's sermon goes, for without doubt that must be an excellent, admirable sermon which He Himself delivers from heaven:

> "This is My beloved Son, in whom I am well pleased." [Matt. 3:17]

This is a brief sermon, and yet so rich and broad that no man on earth can comprehend it or ever be done studying it. For in it the divine Majesty includes and presents all His divine wisdom and understanding, and at the same time pours out all His will and heart, so that all that He is and

---

[39] In place of this word, Rörer's notes here read: "enlightens" (WA 37:272.23).

[40] The following section is adapted mainly from Rörer's notes of Luther's sermon on February 8, 1534 (WA 37:288–93).

has the power to do is made public. Of course, this is infinite and incomprehensible, and yet all bound up here in the briefest form and related to this single person, called Christ. He points us only to Him and can preach about nothing else than this Christ, who is being baptized. In this way He makes and consecrates Him Doctor and Priest, as well as King and Lord of all things, not with rancid chrism,[41] but with the living Holy Spirit, resting visibly upon Him.

Although we cannot undertake to explain this sermon, yet in order that we may discuss it a little, it should first be noted, once again, that these words were not spoken because Christ had need of them any more than this whole revelation happened for His sake. Indeed, He was not made man for His own sake. Rather, it should be understood that it was preached and written for us, even as all of it (His being conceived and born, suffering and rising again) was done for us.

Therefore, we should not let it pass by like a useless, lazy, and cold sermon, and let this glorious testimony be in vain, which really ought to be written in our heart with letters of pure fire, since the high Majesty Himself preaches it to us. What a horrible affliction it is that these words are left lying so cold and dead, and receive no attention, and that no one knows how to apply them! They all think this is an ancient matter that no longer concerns us. They do not read it or hear it in any way different from an account of a Turkish battle or of Dietrich of Bern.[42] But such a cold and lazy approach, by which no one is warmed or kindled and edified, is not what it means to handle the Word of God rightly.

Therefore, (I say,) you should hear and read these words "This is My beloved Son," etc., as if the Father were speaking from heaven this very hour into my heart and yours and saying: "Let all the world turn its ears and hearts this way. I preach nothing else than this Son, nor do I wish anything else to be preached and commanded, nor heard or received (than My words and preaching), so that all eyes and ears may be filled and directed only to cling to the Son." These words will admirably show us what we get from this.

We have, then, two parts to this sermon, as He Himself divides it. The first is: "This is My beloved Son"; the second: "in whom I am well pleased." Now we must not allow the term "My Son" to lead us astray, as the heretics do who say that it is a term of favor and not of nature or true Godhead. They can very cleverly and narrowly assert and conclude (as the Jews do also): "If

---

[41] See above, p. 22 n. 17.

[42] Dietrich of Bern was a heroic figure based loosely on the historical Ostrogothic king Theodoric the Great (454–526); see AE 69:378 n. 5. Many of the stories about Dietrich are not in the least historical; cf. *Large Catechism* (1529) Longer Preface 11 (Kolb-Wengert, p. 381; *Concordia*, p. 354).

God never had a wife in heaven, then He could not have any natural Son. Therefore, Christ must be called a Son of God only as a favor or by choice, just as a man who has no children can adopt someone else's, call him his son, and make him his heir. He is then called not a natural [son] or a born [son], but an adopted son. Even though he is heir of all his possessions, he is still not so by nature, nor of his flesh and blood, but only of his will by which he chose and adopted him."

But we say in accordance with Scripture that Christ is both called and is the Son of God not simply by His will or favor, the way we are called only His adopted and elect children, but is the true, natural Son by true, natural divine birth, of the same divine essence with the Father. For the manner of speaking that He uses here ("This is My Son"), where He speaks only in the singular or calls only one man "His Son," is not found in Scripture otherwise. Rather, when He is talking about other people, it occurs either in the plural, about many, or collectively, as when He uses the term "My son" to mean a whole group, for example: "I brought My son out of Egypt" (Hosea 11 [:1]), that is, the whole nation of Israel. Otherwise He keeps the distinction of never using this term for any single person, neither angel nor man. Thus the Epistle to the Hebrews says, "To which angel did He ever say, 'You are My Son'?" etc. (Hebrews [1:5]). He speaks the same way when He says to David, referring only to Christ: "He shall be My Son, and I will be His Father" [1 Chron. 22:10; 2 Sam. 7:14]. David then introduced this into the Psalter, showing that he took it to mean a true, natural Son. For instance, he says, "I will make Him the firstborn Son, the highest of the kings on the earth" (Psalm 89 [:27]). Likewise, he says, "The Lord said to Me, 'You are My Son. Today I have begotten You,'" etc. (Psalm 2 [:7]). He does not use these words for any other person, even the angels, though they are the highest creatures that God has created and are otherwise referred to as children of God [Job 38:7]. Yet (says the same Epistle, Hebrews [1:5]) He did not honor them with this high title ("My firstborn Son" and "I have begotten You"), but only this person, Christ.

Therefore, we should make our faith firm and certain with this verse and conclude that this Son is something higher than and different from all created things, both in heaven and on earth, since God does not give this name to any other. He must certainly be called a true, natural Son, of the same nature and essence or majesty with the Father, just as a man's son is called a natural son because he is of the same nature or of the same blood and flesh.

Thus this is first spoken about this person whom He shows and points to as the one and only Christ, who is being baptized in the Jordan. He distinguishes Him above all others, and honors and praises Him above all created things by personally proclaiming His name through special revelation. This leads us to conclude emphatically that He must be higher than all angels and, consequently, true God (for there is nothing above and outside of creation but God). Therefore, we should esteem and honor Him as He is depicted and represented by this sermon: a person who is at the same time both true, natural man, and yet not only or merely man but also the true, natural, and hereditary Son of God.[43]

We must embrace and cling to this with faith and dismiss the fools who barge in with reason and quibble and fool around according to their own notions. I could do that as well as any of them, if imagination and fantasies had any validity. But how does that stand up against such clear, strong words, and how can my conscience be assured about their glosses and interpretations? Here they lead me off to an imaginary realm, or else they produce other passages, which they stretch and twist the same way they do with this verse, such as when Scripture says, "There is only one God," etc. [Deut. 6:4]. With this they scream and thunder against us, as though we did not confess the same thing, and it were difficult and unusual for a Christian to say such things.

I am well aware of this, and it is just what we have been saying: there is nothing outside of creation but the one God. But when we go outside and beyond creation into the Majesty and try to know how things operate there, then my wisdom ceases and must listen to what He says about how and what He is. Then I hear Him say that there are three persons in one nature and divine essence. I must remain there, not quibble and say, "Well, I cannot understand it." Therefore, it is invalid to try to use the verse (that there is no more than one God [Deut. 6:4]) against this. All that Moses and Scripture wish to say with it is what we also say when we speak of the essence that is outside of creation: that there is no more than one God and that no one should seek any other God. If I know and believe this, then I must accordingly listen to how this same God speaks of His majesty and interprets or explains who He is. Then I cannot err or make a mistake. So, since I hear from His own word and testimony from heaven that Christ is His true Son and the same God, albeit another person, I should accept this

[43] Rörer's notes here read: "As the son of a man is called natural man because he has his flesh, blood, and nature, so[, says God,] 'He is not chosen but born My Son.' Thus Christ is not a chosen, named, adopted son, but has the same majestic nature as God. This is how to speak properly of this Son, who is a son differently from angels and men. Thus He says, 'You are sons of the Most High, gods' (Psalm 82 [:6]). But He who stands in the Jordan, appears as a man—of Him the Father says, 'He is My natural Son.' Therefore, when He uses the name and has the honor through which He is more highly praised than the highest creature and which He gives to no angel nor man on earth, it must be higher than all angels and creatures. Therefore, He is true God . . . " (WA 37:290.21–29).

as true. It is not mine to search out how it may be and how it accords with logic, but only to believe and speak as I hear Him speak. Therefore, since He calls Him His Son by terms that He uses for no created thing, He must be true and very God.

In this way we also confess this article in our Creed: "I believe in Jesus Christ, His" (the Father's) "only Son," etc.[44] For with the term "only Son," we understand that He is His true, natural Son, begotten of His nature, that is, our Lord, whom we worship and call on (as God), begotten of the Father in eternity, and born of the Virgin in time or according to the human nature, so that two natures are united together in one person and called one Christ. This is what we believe and preach. Whoever does not want to do so, let him abandon it and go on being wise and instructing God how to talk. As for us, we will let Him teach and instruct us, and follow that, even if it does not agree with our own wisdom.

The first thing, then, that we learn here is who this person is—namely, God's only Son—and how He (being His true, begotten heir) was made by Him to be Lord of heaven and earth and all creatures. Thus He is here extolled, proclaimed, and crowned King by the Father Himself, not with purple or gold, nor seated on a golden throne, nor anointed with chrism, as is done to men, but adorned with a different crown and balm: the divine Majesty's proclamation and voice, saying, "This is My beloved Son," etc.—the Lord in heaven and earth, King of all kings and Lord of all lords, etc.

By nature He is already God and Lord of all creation and does not need to have such things stated and proclaimed for His own sake. But it is revealed, explained, and conveyed to us so that we also may know how He should be regarded, and it is preached to us so that we may see that His person (which is here displayed in the human nature) is the foundation of heaven and earth, angel and man, righteousness, life, sin, death, hell, and all that can be named that is not God Himself. Beyond that, this man is appointed and proclaimed that we might believe that we have just such a Lord in Him, and are baptized on the basis that He will be our Lord and govern, protect, and aid us, so that we have all things in Him, and nothing shall harm or overpower us.

But this cannot be expressed by any language, nor decked or adorned with any gold or precious gem. For being called God's natural Son and Lord of all creation is higher than can be measured. One single angel by himself is higher and more powerful than the whole world with all its splendor and power. He, however, is incomprehensibly far and high above all angels and whatever can be thought of in creation, and yet here [He is] completely

[44] The Second Article of the Apostles' Creed (Kolb-Wengert, p. 21; *Concordia*, p. 16).

poured out and given to us in the phrase "This is My beloved Son." But, as I said, this must all be embraced by faith.

For what is said of this Man is too different from what is seen. As great and wonderful a glory as it is to be God's natural Son and Heir, or Lord of all things, so much greater and more wonderful is it for all these things to be placed in this person lying in the Virgin's lap and (in this passage) standing in the Jordan and being baptized. Here there is nothing to see but a poor, wretched, naked Man, who could not look more lowly, devoid of any appearance of glory and authority, and yet He alone is supposed to be called, and believed to be, Lord of all lords, Emperor of all emperors—indeed, of all angels as well—who mightily holds in His hands both world and devil, sin, death, and all things. Who could discern such a thing in this poor Man, or who might be able to say or believe it about Him, if God Himself had not revealed it from heaven and said, "This is He"? This is the first part of this divine sermon from heaven.

The second is: "in whom I am well pleased." With this He also consecrates Him a cleric or priest, just as Psalm 110 [:4] calls Him an everlasting priest, inasmuch as He stands eternally before God to reconcile and represent us [Heb. 7:25]. For we know that we all are born in sin, condemned to death, and forever under the wrath of God, from the first man to the last. The devil caused this and brought it upon the whole human race. Who, then, is able to reconcile us to God and remove the curse from us? No man, no prophet, no saint ever arose who dared to step before God and could quell His wrath. They themselves all had to die from it. Indeed, no angel even was able to take that wrath on himself and make satisfaction for it.

Yet if men were to be helped, anyone saved, sin blotted out, death slain, the devil's kingdom destroyed, hell extinguished, and God's grace brought to light, known, and praised, then He Himself had to undertake it and send and appoint a Mediator by whom we might go from wrath to grace, from sin and death to godliness and life. No one had the power or ability to do this but His only Son, and that was by His coming to us Himself and taking on our nature, blood, and flesh. Nevertheless, if He was to deliver us from sin, He would Himself be born without sin and thus, as Mediator between God and us, be both true God and man. But in order for Him to be received and believed in for that purpose, the Father Himself had to reveal it to us from heaven in this passage and bear witness of Him: "This is My beloved Son, in whom I am well pleased."

In other words, He says here: "If you want to be freed from wrath and condemnation and seek and find favor with Me, you must come here and cling to this Man. He is to be the only true Priest and Mediator. Here and nowhere else will you find your reconciliation and a gracious God. Up until now, under the Law of Moses, there has been a great deal of worship, priests, and sacrifices, and various works and methods among men all done so that God would say, 'This pleases Me.' But none of it was able to achieve this, for they never had this heavenly testimony of His, saying, 'This pleases Me, and because of it I will be gracious and forgive sins,' etc. Rather," He says, "I am pleased with this Man alone. It is My will to be gracious and reconciled through Him. Whatever is to be pleasing and acceptable to Me must flow from Him."

Thus by these words God strips away and excludes all that we could perform and undertake with the intent of obtaining His grace and being saved thereby (whether it be worship, sacrifices, or works undertaken from the Law of Moses or of one's own initiative). All that is pleasing to Him is confined to the Son, so that nothing in addition to and outside the Son avails to appease God. "Whatever He is, speaks, and does, or what is or is spoken or done in Him," God says, "is sure and certain to be heartily pleasing to Me. I have no desire or intention of being pleased in or delighted with any other. All eyes, ears, and hearts are to be turned to Him. There it is all to be: all wrath and hostility canceled and gone, and nothing but grace and love in their place."

Behold, by this voice God thus placed Him in the highest honor of being both His true King and Priest, Heir, and Lord, powerfully reigning and ruling over all things, and at the same time making the Father gracious toward us. With this He shows His fatherly heart for all who believe in Christ, assuring them that God desires not to be their enemy but their gracious, kind Father, who is no longer willing or able to be angry with us or to cast us away (provided we abide in Christ), even if we stumble and fall. When we turn back and cling to this Son, it will all be simply forgiven and forgotten when He says: "This is pleasing to Me for the sake of My dear Son and Priest. This is how I wish to be appeased and made gracious. You have My whole heart." Thus in such brief but fine, unfathomable words He personally enfolds pure grace and consolation and opens up for us a vast heaven full of light and fire, sincere mercy, and fatherly love, with the result that people are not terrified of Him as of an angry judge (as the devil depicts Him to timid, frightened hearts and threatens the hard and impenitent with the Law). Rather, He eagerly desires that we might simply look to Him for all love and good, expect that from Him with a joyful heart, and no longer be afraid of anything that tries to terrify or afflict us.

He gave us this revelation Himself specifically to reassure us and make us certain that, in Christ, His dear Son, He desires to show us pure grace and fatherly love and to maintain these in the face of everything that tries to wrest it away from us. Thus He wishes to have all wrath and guilt canceled, and nothing else to avail, neither the authority and power of any lords, kings, or princes—indeed, of any angels; nor any of the wisdom, holiness, or worship of the world; and, briefly, anything that tries to require something else of us, save only adherence to this Lord and Priest. He will aid us against every hostility and tribulation, terror and affliction and is the eternal Mediator—indeed, the eternal Pledge presented to us by the Father that He will be a gracious and kind Father, provided we do not seek it somewhere else than in the Son to whom He points us (as do those who presume to use the Law or their own invented works to reconcile themselves to God and obtain forgiveness of sins).

In order that we might grasp this gracious heart and will of the Father with more strength and certainty, He illustrated it not only in these words but also in the external sign and action of this manifestation. For He revealed Himself here not as formerly when He founded the old testament and gave the Law through Moses on Mount Sinai, when the whole sky was black and obscured by thick clouds, and nothing was heard or seen but thunder and lightning so that the mountain was issuing smoke, the earth was quaking, and there was nothing but terror and trembling [Exod. 19:16, 18]. Rather, here every place is full of clarity and light and a joyful appearance, so that all is pure heaven, and all creation, a cause of laughter for us. The divine Majesty stoops down to us, so that there is no longer a division between God and ourselves, and shows Himself visibly in the most kind and pleasant form: the Son in His human nature, standing at the water like another, innocent man with His minister John; the Father in that pleasant voice and proclamation which speaks of pure grace and love; and the Holy Spirit confirms this, hovering over Christ with that lovely shape of an innocent dove, which is free from all gall and wrath and has a tender heart. In short, nothing is seen or heard but comforting, tender love, as though heaven were dripping honey and sugar and raining and showering pure grace and mercy, so that we have nothing else to think of or expect from Him.

Whose heart or tongue will fathom the sweet consolation in these words when it believes and feels (as a Christian ought) that God was speaking the words to him: "This is My beloved son, in whom I am well pleased"? This is just as if He were to say to us: "Here I give you all My grace and love and kindness which I have in My heart and powers. In order that you may not doubt, nor be able to, I hereby give you not Moses or a prophet, nor an angel or saint, nor a treasure of gold and silver, nor other great riches of earth or heaven, but My own dear Son. That is, I give you My own heart and the true, eternal spring and source of all grace and good, whom no angel nor created thing in heaven and earth can fathom or comprehend. He is to be the sign and pledge of My grace and love against your sin and terror. Since He is by birth and right the only Heir and Lord of all creation, so in Him you are My children and heirs and have all that He has and possesses." In addition to giving us the right and inheritance which He has by nature, He also, by His suffering and death as our Priest and Bishop, merited and gained for us the state of being forever His elect children and fellow heirs of all His goods. Behold, what more should He do or give, and what could a man's heart desire or imagine higher and better? Yet He does this without any of our merit or cooperation, before any man has asked for it or thought of it, so that we have nothing anywhere to boast of here, but must leave it at pure grace. We are unable to do anything for it, except to thank and praise Him for this indescribable grace. Neither does He desire anything else.

From this you yourself can judge what is being done by those who oppose this divine sermon and revelation by teaching and preaching their own human works and merit, and presume to use these to reconcile both themselves and others to God and to earn grace, as though they did not need the Lord Christ at all and were perfectly able to please God without Him. Indeed, [you yourself can judge] what is merited by our Papists today, who refuse to hear or tolerate this preaching about Christ and Baptism, and who persecute and murder those who preach rightly. What is more fitting for them—since, when they are offered and presented all grace and love in Christ, they wantonly swat it away and refuse to have anything to do with it—than that instead they should have all wrath and no favor, be mercilessly wiped out, and burn in hell forever? Already it is evident that such wrath and chastisement has been determined for them, inasmuch as they steadily continue with their stubborn wickedness and act increasingly worse, so that their ruin is all the more horrible. But may God defend us who have His grace, so that we may acknowledge it, and help us to abide in it!

Let that be enough as a brief discussion of this beautiful text, in which the true beginning of the New Testament and the summary of the whole Gospel is drawn up and given us by God Himself. It is stated so briefly and yet so completely that no man could include or express it so that it is not viewed coldly and passed by as if it were some worthless human invention. For we have seen in it what great and glorious things are written and portrayed for us concerning this most worthy Sacrament of Baptism, and what we are to think about it: how this water was sanctified by Christ when He touched it with His own body and in it opened heaven to us. In it He gives us the whole, entire divine Majesty in person and Himself, displays pure grace and pleasure from the Father in Christ (to whom Baptism belongs), testifies that He will bless and help us, and gives us in exchange for sin the righteousness of God, and in exchange for death eternal life. Since this all happens in connection with the Baptism of Christ, it is thereby clearly shown to us that it is given in and through Baptism, inasmuch as it (as stated) was all revealed in this way not for Christ's sake but for our sake. This happened in the very place where John was baptizing, a region otherwise desolate, to show that He thus intends to honor Baptism, indicating to us what He thinks of it. Otherwise He would have made this revelation in a more notable place, such as in the capital city of Jerusalem and in the temple, etc.

Now you have what there is to say concerning the power and benefit of Baptism, all of which Christ includes and interprets, as shown above, in this one word, when He says, "Whoever believes and is baptized will be *saved*" [Mark 16:16]. For by this He informs us that it is His will and order that we receive Baptism, not in order that the body might be cleansed and remain outwardly pure and clean, as was the ancient Jewish daily purification; nor that it should merely be an empty symbol by which we are recognized, as the Jews were by circumcision; but ultimately in order that by it we might be saved, that is, delivered from sin, death, hell, and every evil, and be eternally righteous, holy, living, and heirs of heaven. All this is the result of this word. For if man is to be saved, it must be preceded by his being purified and justified from sin, since no one is saved except he who is first righteous and holy. Likewise, if he is to be saved, he must also first be delivered from death and have life, and at the same time be secured against hell and damnation, and, finally, have every sort of woe, calamity, sorrow, fear, and dread taken away and be brought to eternal peace and joy. Baptism (I say) brings us all these things not because it is water, but because it contains the name and power of God, who ordained that it be a heavenly, divine water and wants such things to be given by means of these two things: water and Word. He has enough power and strength in His finger (if He wished and ordered it) to accomplish them even through creatures lowlier than water.

Thus you have (I think) sufficient basis for why we praise and exalt Baptism so highly above everything else on earth. From all this you see clearly that in so doing we are not extolling any of our own works, however great or admirable they may be, but only God's work and power, which really should be extolled and praised. Other teachers and preachers, whether the new sectarian spirits or the old papal ass, do not pay heed to it, nor can they, though they, too, certainly have right under their nose the glorious texts and testimonies of Scripture concerning Baptism. But they flit about it as if it were nothing, unable to oppose us except by sputtering, out of their worthless inventions and fantasies, that instead we forbid good works and do not live as we ought (in their opinion). With this they think that they have done well and humiliated us. But let them sputter and spout, for they are not worthy enough that they can or should speak otherwise. But if they were so godly as to be able to or willing to look at Scripture, they would certainly leave our teaching uncontested.

What, then, is all their spouting about works? What business do we have commanding or forbidding works here? Why do they not talk to Christ about it and ask Him to change things? After all, we did not devise or invent the verse "Whoever believes and is baptized," etc. Is it Luther's or the pope's? Obviously it belongs to the Holy Spirit and to Christ Himself and is in the same Bible that both they and we have. In truth, we are not talking about our works here, nor should we be.

Do you yourself say, "What is in Baptism that we can extol as our own? Or what do we add to it?" Of course, I am not suggesting that anyone is so brutish or brash as to say that Baptism is his or anyone's. We do not talk about baptizing in my name or your name or a saint's name, but "in the name of the Father and Son and Holy Spirit." He is the Master who can and will do it. If there is any desire to speak of works, He is the one to be extolled. For He does the true works that deserve to be extolled as works of God: blotting out sin, driving off death, extinguishing hell.

These (I say) are different works from those trifling things that they used to talk about, such as monasticism, works of their own choosing, fasting, going on a pilgrimage barefoot, holding and endowing Masses—all of which they propounded not only apart from God's Word but also to the despite and scorn of Baptism, indeed, to the terrible defaming of God's name and His works, meanwhile exalting and extolling their own works as equal to Baptism. Their teachers shamelessly write: "If anyone enters a monastery and takes holy orders, it is just as if he emerged from Baptism that very moment."[45]

This is the blasphemous preaching and true archabomination with which the pernicious Antichrist has filled Christianity and led the people from Baptism to our own works—indeed, violently torn them away from Baptism and put their own works in place of Christ and His Baptism, with the result that no one was able to keep it except those whom God miraculously sustained in it. For no sooner had we taken off the children's shoes,[46] and they had emerged from the blessed font, than they [the Papists] took it all away by this preaching: "You lost Baptism and soiled your christening gown[47] long ago by sinning; so now you have to think about repenting of your sin and making satisfaction for it by fasting, praying, going on

[45] See Thomas Aquinas (ca. 1225–74), *ST*, 2.2., q. 88 art. 6 (Blackfriars 39:175).

[46] I.e., grown up. The saying is explained in Wander 2:1330, "Kinderschuh" no. 4.

[47] The christening gown is the white robe traditionally placed on a child after Baptism, retained in Luther's baptismal liturgies as well: see *Order of Baptism* (1523), AE 53:100–101; and *Order of Baptism Newly Revised* (1526), AE 53:109.

pilgrimages, and making endowments until you are reconciled to God and so return to His favor."

Thus with one blow all that we had received through Baptism is crushed and annihilated, tragically fulfilling what St. Peter prophesied to them in 2 Peter 2 [:20–22], that by their doctrine those who barely escaped error and were cleansed from sin through Baptism became involved and entangled again in their former filth and drowned in it. They act just like the sow that, leaving the pond, wallowed in the next puddle. The same thing happened to us through the pope's teaching and all the books and writings of his theologians and decretalists,[48] who all did nothing else than to dishonor and defame Christ and His Baptism so that no one was able to rejoice or take comfort in it.

I myself was a monk for fifteen years, not counting the life I lived before that, when I was careful to read all their books and do all that I could, but I could never once find comfort in my Baptism. I kept thinking: "Now, when are you going to amend your ways and make satisfaction so that you obtain a gracious God?" By such thoughts I was driven to monasticism, and afflicted and tortured myself with fasting, freezing, and a strict life, and yet I accomplished nothing thereby except to lose Baptism—indeed, to help deny it. This is the fruit and reward that we owe to their teaching of works, which they still defend and know of nothing else to cry about than works, contrary to the preaching of Christ and His Baptism, which God Himself gave from heaven. Thus they in fact cancel Christ's Baptism and establish in its place a baptism of works, so that by virtue of their doctrine they are as harmful as the Anabaptists. Indeed, they make nothing but Jews or Turks out of us, as if we were unbaptized.

Therefore, lest we be led astray by such things, let us keep this teaching pure, as we see and grasp it here, that Baptism is not our work or doing; let us preserve a great and vast distinction between God's works and our own. There are some works which the divine Majesty does in us, such as creating us with body and soul and giving us all that is in heaven and earth. These are His common works toward all men on earth, and all is very admirable and good. In addition to these works He does others for those who become Christians and His children. After we fall through sin and are ruined, He takes us back into His divine hands, gives us His Word and Baptism, thereby cleansing and purifying us from sin. These (I say) are the works belonging only to the divine Majesty. We add nothing to this, nor do we have any power except to receive and accept it from Him. When we want to speak of

---

[48] Decretalists are commentators on the *Decretals*, the official collection of medieval canon law, gathered from papal bulls, decrees, letters, and conciliar decisions under Pope Gregory IX (r. 1227–41) and extended by his successors.

great, divine works, these are the works about which to boast. For God is the true Master of works. He can blot out sin, slay death, defeat the devil, overthrow hell, etc., all with His finger.

Now after we have obtained and acknowledged these works of God, let us also talk about works that we can and should do, namely, thanking and praising God before all the world for His works in us so that others may also see and receive it. Thus we can live to the glory of God and the benefit of our neighbor, help everyone, and serve with body, property, and whatever means we have. When we do this, we do not teach and praise our good works as a means to go to heaven. The reason why they should be done is not that they should serve us, blot out sin, overcome death, and acquire heaven, but for the benefit and need of our neighbor.

Thus these two things are rightly divided when they are separated from each other as far and wide as heaven and earth are from each other. For God's works come down from above and give us purely heavenly, eternal benefits, whereas our own works remain here below and produce only what pertains to this earthly life and existence. The coarse Papists know nothing of this distinction, which is nonetheless correct and clear. They spew forth a great deal about works, but have no idea what it means to teach or to forbid good works; they brew and blend them together so that no one knows what is God's work and what is ours. In fact, they completely obscure and abandon them, set up human works instead, and thus pervert and corrupt the true doctrine everywhere.

III.

Up to now there has been sufficient discussion of both what Baptism is and what power and benefit it has. It would now be appropriate to talk about its use or about those who receive it. For this is where things diverge and the disparity begins, in that not all receive the same power and benefit from Baptism even though they receive the same Baptism. There are two kinds of people who receive it: those with faith and those without faith. Therefore, though the Baptism in itself is proper and remains the same for one as for another, and as good, holy, and divine for the unbeliever as for the one who believes, yet a great difference appears among them in that the unbeliever does not enjoy its power and benefit, which is not the fault of Baptism but his own for not receiving and applying it as he should. The vessel is not ready to receive it, since the heart is shut, and Baptism's power cannot enter it and work in it, for the heart does not desire it or want it.

It is the same way with the physical creation. The sun shines and gives light every place, and yet not all see it or are warmed by it. Yet it is just as much the true sun with its brightness, light, heat, and all its power for one man as for all. Why, then, does it remain dark and cold for these people? Because they have shut their doors and windows and are unwilling and unable to see the sun. Unbelieving hearts are the same. Although they receive true Baptism, a divine, heavenly washing, and all that God has in it, yet, since they will neither believe in it nor accept it, it does them no good—not because of their inability or imperfection, but because they turn their back and do not open their heart, that it might work its power therein.

So, by contrast, he who believes that in Baptism God has appointed for him a washing of new birth by which he is cleansed from sin and becomes a child of God, etc., receives and finds it as he believes. In his case the heart is open, and Baptism enters with all its power, giving light and warmth, and out of an old, dead man makes a new, living saint.

Christ also shows this difference in these words: "Whoever believes and is baptized will be saved, but whoever does not believe will be condemned" [Mark 16:16]. For in these words He includes the purpose of Baptism, or what it is supposed to work, and attaches to that how those in whom it is to accomplish its work should be ready, or else what is required in order that it be received profitably, namely, faith.

There has been frequent discussion elsewhere concerning how Baptism should be used, namely, that faith should always cling to it and be active as long as we live. At present let it suffice that we learn to keep the proper distinction (which we touched on above)[49] against the erring spirits, that it is one thing to receive true Baptism and another thing to get its power and benefit. We are not to reject and despise Baptism, even if it is not rightly received. The Anabaptists do this when they assert that the Baptism of the Papists is invalid because it is both given and received without faith, and those who were baptized by them must be baptized anew. Long ago, too, this error troubled many people in Christendom, as I mentioned above regarding St. Cyprian.[50]

In our quarrel with the Papists over Baptism and the Sacrament,[51] it is not our meaning that their Baptism and Sacrament (provided they are conducted according to God's order) are wrong or have no power. Rather, we reproach their doctrine as contrary to faith and the true use of Baptism, by which they render Baptism incapable of imparting its power, and pry it away from those who are rightly baptized, and (as much as they can) let no one keep it pure. This they do by saying that it is good for nothing once the christening gown[52] has been soiled and innocence lost; rather, the sin

---

[49] See above, pp. 48–49.

[50] See above, pp. 21–22.

[51] I.e., Baptism and the Sacrament of the Altar (the Lord's Supper).

[52] See above, pp. 47–48 and n. 47 there.

(committed after Baptism) must be blotted out by our works of repentance and satisfaction. Thus they substitute our works for holy Baptism and also set up a rebaptism not by water but by works. As said above, they have even shamelessly equated their monastic life with Baptism.[53]

It is against such slanderous and damned doctrine that we preach and fight. Yet we do not therefore deny the Baptism which we have from them, but we do just the opposite, restoring it (which in the name of Christendom they received from Christ through the apostles) to its proper use, contrary to their false teaching of the baptism of works (by which they destroy Christ's Baptism), so that its power may be recognized and retained. Similarly, we purified and brought to light the Gospel and Scripture, which they received quite correctly but obscured—indeed, perverted and falsified—them with their human doctrines. The Anabaptists do not retain this distinction, so that they might separate the Baptism which the pope gives in Christ's name from their doctrine that they have devised contrary to Baptism. Rather, they condemn both the doctrine and the Baptism as being nothing and as counting for nothing, as though it were a worthless human invention made up by them (as their doctrine is), and thereby take Baptism from us completely.[54]

That we may therefore retain Baptism and the true doctrine over against the deception of both the pope and the Anabaptists, let us always teach and use this distinction between the two things, that is, God's work and ours. When we talk about what Baptism is and what benefit it has in itself, we are not talking about our works. Who will say that he created or invented Baptism, or that he would know anything about it if God Himself had not instituted and commanded it for us (let alone that we should be able to give it its power and benefit)? Therefore, regarding both its essence and its power, it is entirely and completely God's work, and we do not add a single thing to it, nor are we able to. We are, furthermore, not to regard or ask what we do or do not do here, but when we see it treated according to His Word and command, we are by no means to doubt that he who is being baptized has received true Baptism. However, after you have received it, it is upon you to make sure that you believe and use Baptism properly. Then we are talking about our deeds. In short, these two matters (I say), Baptism and faith, should be separated as far as heaven is from earth and as God from man.

The works that God makes and does are firm, certain, unchangeable, and eternal, just as He Himself is unchangeable and eternal. Therefore, they stand and abide, firm and unfailing, and never become something else, even

[53] See above, pp. 47–48.

[54] The following section is mainly adapted from Rörer's notes of Luther's sermon on February 2, 1534 (WA 37:278–84).

if they are completely misused. The things that we do, on the other hand, are unsteady and uncertain, just as we also are, so that nothing can be based or built on them. Therefore, in order that Baptism may stand firm and be certain for us, He did not base it on our faith, since that is uncertain and may well be false, but on His Word and order so that it must be and remain true, and not grow any weaker or less significant even if faith is not present.

According to this distinction, then, everyone is able to judge and refute all sorts of error that may arise against Baptism, as indicated above. For instance, there are some who say that Baptism does not count if it is administered by one who does not believe. This has a fine glow to it and made deep incursions long ago, so that even the great bishop and martyr St. Cyprian was taken captive by it. At the time they used the verse from Jesus Sirach [Ecclus. 34:4]: "He who has unclean hands, how shall he make clean? Whatever he touches will also become unclean." So if the Baptism is administered by an unclean priest, or an unbeliever, how can he make him who receives it clean?[55]

But this is basing Baptism on men and making it entirely uncertain—indeed, in vain. If I am supposed to wait until I am assured that he who is baptizing is clean, neither I nor anyone else would ever be baptized. Indeed, I would have to do away with the Our Father, in which we all must say, "Forgive us our debts," etc. [Matt. 6:12].

We say this so that it may by no means get to the point where we let ourselves be directed and led to our own worthiness or the cleanness of our hands. We have other hands here instead of our own, namely, those of Christ, who is completely clean and holy and makes all that He touches holy and clean. He is the one who creates and gives Baptism, and all that occurs in Baptism is His work. So since He to whom Baptism belongs, and who does the baptizing, is clean and remains so, what do I care whether I and you and all men are unclean? My Lord Christ and His Baptism will not be stained by that. The sun is not stained and made unclean by shining as clearly on dung and filth as on gold, but shines just as brightly on a pile of manure as on a white veil and is not diminished in any way, even though that which it touches and on which it works is unclean. So, too, even if Baptism is given by an unclean minister, it will in no way damage Baptism or me, who receive it, since Baptism and the office belong not to man but to Christ.

If it were granted, moreover, that God's order and command are not in force unless the person by whom it is to be performed is clean and without sin, no one could ever preach God's Word or teach, comfort, and govern others, etc., for there will never be anyone who is completely clean and has no need to pray the Our Father. In fact, children would even have to be

---

[55] See above, pp. 21–22, 50.

taught thus: "Why do you want to obey your father or mother? They are not clean or holy!" Likewise, all lords and princes would have to abdicate their office and forbid obedience and rebuke their authority and rule as unclean, since by and large they are ungodly. A fine and laudable government that would be!

Therefore, you see that this is a pernicious error, and God must have sustained the holy martyr Cyprian in an extraordinary way and cleansed him from error by the blood of the Lord Christ. Nevertheless, something harmful was established by this, because from there rebaptism first arose, and is now gaining ground again, so that land and city are being brought into such misery by the worthless illusion of their assertion: "You did not believe when you were baptized, and even if you believed, those who administered Baptism to you were unclean and ungodly, which means you must have yourselves baptized anew," etc.

Therefore, whoever is unwilling to be deceived, let him hold to this doctrine by which he is able to speak about it distinctly, and say: "My being baptized is not my work, nor that of him who gave it to me, for it is not described as mine or the priest's or any man's, but Christ my Lord's Baptism, and neither my cleanness nor yours may add a thing to it. It is not for me or any man to sanctify and cleanse Baptism, but we are all to be sanctified and cleansed by Baptism. Thus I will not base Baptism on my faith, but, on the contrary, my faith will be based and built on Baptism."

I will regard it as the same whether the one being baptized, whether young or old, believes or not. It is entirely possible that a Jew may have himself baptized to deceive us Christians. In that case, I could not say that his Baptism is nothing because he is a scoundrel and mocks Baptism. On the contrary, I would have to say that he has received true holy Baptism, albeit to his harm and condemnation. I cannot say that if an unbeliever slanders God's name, he does not slander the true God. Likewise, I cannot say that the Gospel is not the true Word of God even when the one preaching or hearing it is a scoundrel. So, too, the true, most worthy Sacrament of Christ's body and blood was received by the traitor Judas as well as by St. Peter. God does not change for our sake and will not alter His Word and works, or let them weaken, through our belief or unbelief.[56] For this much is true: that we are not clean because of ourselves, nor can we remain so. If Baptism depended on our purity or faith, it would be in a sorry state indeed, and the devil would promptly snatch our faith away and destroy Baptism so that no one could ever be certain of it or rely on it.

---

[56] Rörer's notes here add: "Otherwise it would follow that he who takes Christ's Sacrament unworthily does not receive the Sacrament" (WA 37:279.25–26).

I am eager to hear from an Anabaptist what answer they can give when someone asks them why they baptize; since they reject our Baptism and rebaptize those who were (as they say) "improperly" baptized before, how will they make certain that their Baptism is proper? If they can do that, I will have myself rebaptized, not only once but also as often as they like. "Well," they say, "you were baptized previously and do not know whether you believed. But now I baptize you because you believe and know what you are doing."

But how do you know whether the one being baptized truly believes even now? "From the fact," they say, "that he confesses his faith and asks for Baptism." That is what you call building on the same sand as before. How do you become certain that he is not deceiving you with his confession? If his saying so is enough, any villain might well say so and act as if he believes. If you put your trust in that, I will finally counter you from the Scriptures that all men are liars and false [Ps. 116:11], and putting trust in men is frequently forbidden [cf. Ps. 146:3; Isa. 2:22; Jer. 17:5]. Thus all your business with rebaptizing is made uncertain—indeed, not merely uncertain but also forbidden and damnable, since a work which belongs to the divine Majesty is founded on men, and, contrary to God, [your rebaptizing] places faith or trust in a created thing.

We, however, will build not at all on man's work but strictly on God's, which is not only certain and neither fails nor deceives but also, once done, lasts and avails forever. It never needs to be changed or renewed the way men's deeds and ways change and shift. Take, for instance, the patriarchs in the Old Testament, who also had a baptism, which was the Ten Commandments. As St. Paul says, "They were baptized with the cloud into Moses" (1 Corinthians 10 [:2]), that is, in the Ten Commandments, on the basis of which God made a covenant with them through Moses. Yet there were many thousands among them who did not believe but practiced idolatry, blasphemed God, and rebelled, etc. Should they have said therefore that the Ten Commandments were obsolete, and God could make some different ones? Or when David had his terrible fall into both adultery and murder, should he have said therefore that the Fifth and Sixth Commandments were void and God had to give him others? Then He would have to make another Ten Commandments for the world every single moment.

But the fact is: God's Commandments are and remain eternally. Even if we fall away from them and do not keep them, and all the world goes to the devil, they will not fall away, but the requirement and duty to keep them remains regardless, no matter how often and how low we fall. We are obliged to keep them continually, just as in other ordinances of God. Princely authority, rule, and law are not weakened when a prince has many disloyal and disobedient subjects in his principality. It is the same with Baptism, by which, once we have received it, we are included and inducted into the number of those who will be saved, and God makes an everlasting covenant of grace with us. The fact that we then often fall and stumble does not render Baptism void. Rather, just as grace lasts and governs forever, as Psalm 117 [:2] says—so that, even though we fall, we can always come back to it (provided we do not deny or oppose it)—so also Baptism lasts forever, and you cannot fall so far away and so far down from it that you cannot and should not take hold of it again. For that reason there is no need for Him to make a new Baptism for you, even if you did not believe. It is (as stated) an eternal washing in which we are placed once and must abide eternally or be forever condemned.

Thus you see that the Anabaptists are blind fools and deceivers who understand nothing about God's Word and works. They sin doubly against holy Baptism: first, through their teaching they slander and condemn true Baptism; second, they give no one a sure Baptism, and thereby have in truth no Baptism. Rather, their baptizing is all a matter of deceit. This one sin is all too serious and terrible, by which they deny and defame true Baptism and thereby bring upon themselves a terrible damnation, since they defiantly oppose God's order and work and so rob both themselves and others of blessed Baptism and all the grace given therein.

Let this suffice for now as a discussion of this most worthy Sacrament of Holy Baptism, so that the pure Christian doctrine and proper understanding of it may be retained in the face of the devil's battalions which he has arrayed against Baptism in order to take it away completely or at least to rob people of its power and benefit. Now we (who by God's grace have the doctrine and use of Baptism pure and undefiled) also need a sermon of our own concerning the fruit and consequence of Baptism, for we perceive a great deficiency among ourselves in this area.

Now, I have often said that a distinction should be made between doctrine and life. The factions both of the Anabaptists and the Papists fall from doctrine and take away either the natural essence of Baptism or else the right use of it. We who have the Gospel, however, praise and honor Baptism as God's work and order and do not (God be praised!) sin against the doctrine and God's Word. Everything is pure and undefiled in the pulpit and in practice as well, since we baptize and are baptized according to them. Where we deserve reproach, however, is in our failure to have our life follow our doctrine. When doctrine and faith are right, the fruit thereof should also follow: that we live a life worthy of Baptism and thereby bear witness that we have not received it in vain. For what good would it do you to have God's Word and command with a right, clear understanding, if you did not act accordingly? So, even if we do not rail against Baptism, we are not helped by our failure to show our faith and live as a baptized person ought to live. Yet this fault with regard to life is to be sharply distinguished from the sin against the doctrine. Here something can still be done, and the life can be improved. But if the doctrine is false, there is no help or hope for the life either, but both are lost and condemned.

This situation is like that of a citizen in a city who can commit two different sins against his superior. For instance, he might disobey his mayor, act against his orders, and thereby fall under his punishment, yet all the while admit that he was doing wrong thereby. It is in this way that these two things, *jus et factum*, "law and obedience to the law," or (as we say here) doctrine and life, can be distinguished. For this transgressor or disobedient person still confesses the law and allows the command to stand. But if he decided to go off and oppose the commandment, did not accept the law, refused to admit wrongdoing, but even went so far as to defend his actions—that would be quite another matter and would not be described as disobedience or transgression, but sedition and *crimen laesae maiestatis*,[57] since he would be directly defying those over him, batting the law aside, and wishing to be the law himself. This calls not for normal punishment from Master Hans,[58] but for the earth to open beneath him and swallow him up, as it did Korah, Dathan, and Abiram (Numbers 16 [:32]).

This world, too, cannot stand it when sin does not want to be sin but wants to be called law—not punished, but affirmed and praised. This is what our good Papists do now. They knowingly persecute the acknowledged truth of the Gospel, try by force to defend their ungodliness, shamelessly contradict God to His face, and say that what He says is nothing and that what they say and do, rather, is to be called the law, so that His Word and command are invalid until it pleases them. This is the very definition of knocking God from His throne and opposing Majesty. The sect of the Anabaptists does the same with holy Baptism, waging sacrilegious war against God's order and making another in its place. This calls not for a sword or temporal punishment but for the devil himself and eternal hellfire.

God preserve us from such sin (even as He does)! For in it there can be no grace or forgiveness, since they fight directly against these things. Yet since we are so graced as to have the doctrine correctly held among us, we should also make sure that our lives conform to it, and not abuse this grace or let it be in vain. But having died to sin and become new people through Baptism, we are to walk henceforth in a new life as newborn people, as Saints

[57] The *crimen laesae maiestatis* ["crime of offended majesty"], known also as "lèse-majesté," is a capital offense against the authority or dignity of a sovereign ruler.

[58] I.e., the executioner.

Peter and Paul exhort [1 Pet. 2:24; Rom. 6:4], so that it may be discerned in our life that we have received Baptism to our benefit and blessing.

Here it is apparent how the devil obstructs us at every turn so that, while Baptism is not treated incorrectly, it nevertheless remains without fruit among us. Although it was without our works and good life that we found grace to obtain Baptism correctly, we are still to devote ourselves to honoring and adorning it with words and works and our whole life from now on. Baptismal fonts, altars, and pulpits are there to remind us of this. Since they are to bear witness to the fact that we are baptized and Christians, we should also plan to honor the baptismal font and so live that we may view it with joy and that it may not bear witness against us.

But tragically, many now act as if they might as well always remain as before in their old skin, live as they please, and so make their glorious Baptism only a covering for their shame, as though they had been called to the kingdom of grace in order to have the power to do as they wish. Despite this, they assure themselves that God is gracious and make the excuse: "I am a weak man. Surely God will take this into consideration and forgive me," etc.[59]

No, not so, dear brother! I did not point you down that path so that Baptism should grant the liberty to sin. Quite the opposite![60] Your sins have been remitted, and you have now come into favor (who were before in disfavor because of sin) so that you might now live another life and depart from sin. Being baptized and remaining in sin do not go together. It is given for the very purpose of taking sin away so that man would become just and increase in good works. If he was disobedient, angry, spiteful, unfaithful, and unchaste before, he is to depart from that, pray an Our Father instead, and from that point on take care and strive to be obedient, patient, and kind. If you do not do this, do not think that all is well with you nor boast about the grace of Christ a great deal in order to justify your sin.

It would certainly be significant, if you should find yourself so greatly improved that, for a year or two or some length of time, you would not become angry, curse, etc., as before. Then, if you should fall once or twice through oversight or weakness, people could take this into consideration and offer you encouragement again. But remaining in your former ways and persisting in being angry, impatient, and spiteful shows that you have received your holy Baptism to your great harm.

---

[59] Rörer's notes here read: "adultery, fornication, scraping, scratching [after money], coercing [a debtor to pay], all wicked tricks. And afterward [they] run to the Sacrament, and you tell me to preach that you are in the kingdom of grace" (WA 37:283.9–10).

[60] *das blat umbgekeret*, literally, "Turn the page!" Similar expressions are explained in *DWB*, s.v. "Blatt" 3.

Likewise, if you had been an adulterer, fornicator, or coveter, then Baptism should teach you from that point on not to strike, commit adultery, covet, steal, and rob any longer. The former is forgiven and dead, and from that point on there is to be a different, just, righteous, beneficent, disciplined man.[61] If you find such life and fruits in yourself for a length of time, it is a sign that Baptism has taken effect in you. If it should happen that you go amiss in one or two things, which would be called falling and stumbling, you may take comfort in grace and forgiveness; yet not in such a way that you would remain lying in it or continue and keep saying: "What can I do about it? I cannot get rid of it. Anyway, all is grace and forgiveness," etc. He will not tolerate that, for thereby you only anger God and go farther and farther from grace until you lose it entirely and finally fall under punishment, even into the accursed sin whereby you despise and slander Baptism and grace, as do the devil's factions.

Consider your own life, therefore, and see how it accords with Baptism, and know that even though you have been called and placed into the kingdom of grace and made a partaker through Christ of all that Christians have, yet if you always remain as before, it cannot be beneficial to you, since you are not honoring your Baptism or keeping it pure. While you might be called a Christian, you have let go of Christ, sin is your lord, you are serving the devil, and you have no more than the name and appearance of Christianity by which you deceive yourself and do yourself harm. As I said before, He not only gave this Baptism and Sacrament for the purpose of forgiving and washing away sin by it but also wishes thereby to purge every day whatever sin still remains, and blot it out completely, so that we become quite a different kind and manner of people, inclined and equipped for every good work. Where it has been rightly received, sin will surely be found to decrease and diminish daily. Where it is not, the opposite appears, so that, while you may have put on the wedding garment, there is filth under it with which you soil it and forfeit its beauty.[62]

---

[61] Rörer's notes here read: "While it is a true Baptism, Sacrament, and Gospel, yet this Sacrament, as Paul [says], is unworthily [taken] [1 Cor. 11:29]. 'If I was a thief, murderer, fornicator,' the baptized ought to say, 'it is no longer valid to rob, steal, fornicate, misbehave. I am to be disciplined, that body, ears, and members become chaste, and not take from others, but help them' " (WA 37:283.21–25).

[62] Rörer's notes here add: "Although the sin is not as great as that of those who deny Baptism, since you speak rightly, yet the life is not present. So many are so much better than the sects, but it is not enough. It is a sign that Baptism has not attained to its power, since you have it without faith, since you do not show faith with any fruit. Therefore, let us not be deceived by ourselves. It is necessary for us to repel the sects, that we may retain the doctrine and Sacrament. Afterward, we must ensure that sins which follow and dishonor the Sacrament are rebuked" (WA 37:284.5–12).

If we want to have this glorious grace, it is necessary that we adorn Baptism and hold it high as a noble, beautiful jewel. This "adornment" is our living a life above reproach. Thus St. Paul teaches (Titus 2 [:10]) servants and [those in] other estates to live in such a way as to adorn the salutary doctrine in all things. How? By being obedient, not dealing dishonestly, not working mischief, etc. This is the beautiful wreath which adorns Baptism, gives it a good reputation and acclaim before everyone, and testifies to us that we have received it fruitfully and are true Christians. By contrast, whoever does not live in his estate as he ought dishonors and disgraces both his own doctrine and his Baptism, and bears witness against himself that he is unworthy of grace and is no more than a blot and stain upon Christians, as Peter ([2] Peter 2 [:20]) calls such people.[63]

Therefore, let us earnestly and diligently seek to be found among those who also embellish and adorn this high treasure of ours with their life and conduct, that we may joyfully boast in these before God and all the world and not be ashamed. Then we will not end up like the others who have lost Baptism. All that they taught and did, or still teach and live, has become futile—indeed, damning to them—and now they are seven times worse off than before [Luke 11:26]. Because they have abandoned this treasure, it is their fitting punishment that they are now hopelessly deceived by all kinds of false doctrine; because they did not pay heed to doing true good works to the glory of Baptism, they must now be driven and afflicted with false good works and do all that the devil wants through his deceivers. The same can happen to us also if we are not concerned and vigilant to avoid losing this precious treasure of the Word and blessed Baptism. He who gave it can also have it taken away again, even as the devil seeks and endeavors to do with all diligence.

Let that be enough as a brief admonition for ourselves, for we must use preaching both to refute false doctrine and to rebuke sin, so that both doctrine and life may proceed correctly and so abide. Amen.

---

[63] Rörer's notes here add: "So for the villager [and] the townsman: if you want to have grace, remember to honor, that is, that your life may be honorable, as one baptized; deal faithfully with your neighbor; do no one wrong. Then you are honoring Baptism, and the works follow. Then you can hope to honor and praise the doctrine not only [by words] but also by your works. Therefore, do not make Baptism a covering for shame, as Paul says, 'perverting the grace of Christ' [Jude 4], that is, that they may do what they like. You were not called to the Gospel for that reason. But Baptism is to take away sin; rather, also to sweep out the relics. Therefore, no hatred, envy, greed, pride, impatience, etc., ought to arise, but be mortified. If it does not, then Baptism is harmful to you. You have, God be praised, the true and pure Gospel, Baptism, grace, and knowledge of Christ" (WA 37:284.18–27).

CHAPTER THREE

SERMONS ON HOLY BAPTISM (1538)

First Sermon on Holy Baptism, on the Second Sunday after Epiphany January 20, 1538

Last[1] time, we said that from this Sunday until Shrove Tuesday we would be preaching on holy Baptism so that we could have a true and correct understanding of it in the Christian Church, especially since the devil is attacking and assailing Baptism so fiercely through the Anabaptists. That is why you should be armed and equipped against him and his scales[2] or members. However, I always wish to begin by reading the text of the Gospel.[3]

Let us now speak about Baptism. Holy Scripture teaches that we are all born in original sin and Adam's fall, which the devil instigated in Paradise, corrupting our flesh and blood, so that we are not only begotten from poisoned seed but also condemned to death, with the result that it might have

[1] Translated by Matthew Carver from Martin Luther, *Dr. Martin Luther's Sämmtliche Werke*, 2nd series, vol. 20, part 1, ed. Ernst Ludwig Enders (Frankfurt am Main: Heyder & Zimmer, 1880), pp. 20–29. The sermons are numbered differently in the editions of Enders and Buchwald (see below, p. 73 n. 19). Cf. the stenographic notes for this sermon in WA 46:145–51 (Aland Pr 1693).

[2] Luther often used the imagery of the devil as a dragon and of Christ as the Christians' knight. The "devil's scales" is explained elsewhere by Luther as "the pope and the bishops" (*Lectures on Galatians* [1531], AE 26:97) or as "pope, bishops, tyrants" (*Commentary on Psalm 110* [1535], AE 13:246).

[3] The Gospel reading was from Luke 2 (WA 46:145, apparatus for line 5), probably vv. 42–52, the traditional Gospel reading for the First Sunday after Epiphany (*Register der Episteln und Evangelien* [1526], WA DB 7:537), about 12-year-old Jesus in the temple. (Luther does not preach on that text here, however.) In 1538, Luther switched the Gospel readings for the First and Second Sundays after Epiphany. The week before, January 13, he had preached on marriage, the theme of the Second Sunday after Epiphany with its Gospel reading from John 2:1–12 (WA 46:139–44).

been better if no man was born. But such is not God's desire, for He says, "Increase and multiply, and fill the earth" [Gen. 1:28]. Yet at the same time we must be aware that our first birth brings with it sin and death, as we see by the fact that all people die. Against this sin and death, God has given this blessed medicine and aid, that those who are born of flesh and blood may become holy and not remain in sin but be born anew and raised up to an immortal, eternal life—as Adam himself was created. On account of our first birth, we are condemned for our sin; yet we are renewed, born again, and healed by the Son of God, who was soon promised to Adam and Eve in Paradise, that the Seed of the woman would crush the serpent's head. Likewise, when He said, "I will put enmity between the serpent and the Seed of the woman" [Gen. 3:15], a Seed or man was promised who would not be conceived in sin or deserving of death and yet would be true man. This Seed was to heal the injury which the serpent had wrought. And so it was. Then God made the whole world to wait, and caused the prophets to point and lead people to that Seed and continually to preach that this Seed was coming and would be born. And so they all pointed to this blessed Seed and were all saved by Him, and mention was made of a time when this Seed, the Savior of the world, would come. Then when He comes, He saves us, who are born in sin and sentenced to death, and restores us to blessedness,[4] and sits down at the right hand of His heavenly Father. Yet He has left behind some signs[5] of His mercy in which He may be recognized and discovered, which are the sacraments of Baptism and the Supper; likewise, the preaching office—which might well be called such, since "Eucharist" includes confession.[6] Absolution, too, belongs to the preaching office—indeed, is a part of the preaching office, since it is a private sermon delivered to each person individually.

Whoever, then, wishes to be released from the fall and escape original sin and death, let him remember to stick with these. Now in our day we do not see how Christ died and rose from the dead. This is why He has left three signs—[each one being] a holy, spiritual sign—which indicates and gives this. God instituted these signs; they are His ordinance: namely, Baptism, the Supper, and the preaching office. It is therefore very important for us to know, first of all, where Baptism comes from, so that no one thinks that it is a thing of man or that Baptism was devised and invented by the will of man, any more than the Supper arises from man's choosing or opinion. Neither are we to view the preaching office as a work of man. Whoever views it as

---

[4] *Seligkeit*, or "salvation."

[5] *Zeichen*, or "tokens."

[6] *Eucharistia* (εὐχαριστία), a traditional term for the Lord's Supper, literally means "thanksgiving."

such is in error and on his way to the devil, as is the pope with his indulgences and purgatory. Rather, the sacraments were instituted and ordained by God because He desired to heal this injury through them. But the pope would have liked God's institution to vanish and these sacred signs to be seen no more, in favor of the Papists' rubbish and rot. Becoming a monk was supposed to count for more than partaking of all the sacraments.[7] Thus blasphemously and wickedly they taught that Baptism was a common, everyday thing, but taking up the cowl was far greater than Baptism, the Supper, and the preaching office put together. Hence people's hearts were directed and taught to view the sacraments as if they had been given only by men. Even without this, human nature is entirely too weak to honor God's Word and the Sacrament, and things have gone so far today that people cannot look at God's Word or regard it as God's Word, especially when it chastises. Then they quickly say, "I am being dishonored!" But our doctrine is not from our own thoughts, but from the ancient institution of God, namely, the preaching of the Gospel, Baptism, the Supper, and confession. We have wiped it clean and purified it of the filth with which the pope besmeared it.

Therefore, take great care to learn what God's institution and man's imagination are. They go around in houses and temporal government, passing statutes and ordinances, common law and custom. So be it. But in the Church of God, which Christ redeemed with His blood and called after His own name, having purchased her with His own body and blood, we must not meddle, but leave it in peace, and offer people the Word of God in its purity along with the sacraments, and woe to those who do not! I have enough to worry about with my own sins. There is no need for me to burden myself with the sins of others, as the pope has done with his indulgence, so that all the sins that have resulted from that are now lying on his head. Were I aware of having this sin of leading so many people astray, I could not bear to live another hour. He has also commanded monks and nuns to remain virgins; yet what sins have been committed in monasteries and convents! The papacy is a veritable brothel in which they lead a shameless life, to say nothing of other detestable and atrocious sins. Truly, the pope is entirely to blame! The sin falls on the pope, bishops, and princes, who still protect and defend these things today. Therefore, it is a fearful thing to live under the papacy and join in the sins which they commit. And the Lord Christ says (Matthew 23:35) that all the blood from Abel to this day would come upon them; and all that sin will also come upon him who joins them in such abominations.

Learn, therefore, to recognize and distinguish God's institution and the things which men institute, and do not be deceived by their holy appearance,

[7] See above, pp. 47–48.

especially in clothing and food. Only look to see whether God has instituted it. If not, say, "Out with it! Keep such filth away from the flock which Christ redeemed with His precious blood. We have the preaching of the Gospel, Baptism, and the Supper. God established these signs for us. Wherever these sacraments are found, Christ says, 'Even though you are conceived in sin and fell into sin through Adam, come and turn away from the serpent's head, the devil, to this sign. Here you will find Me and know that through this sign I will bring help and remedy for the fall.'" View it, therefore, as a divine sign, and remember what we were in the papacy—namely, blind and foolish—and what those of us did who walked to Santiago, Grimmenthal, and Aachen.[8] These things were done in order that by such works we might be reconciled with God. And at once the pope appeared, saying, "I hereby give you an indulgence for this and forgive both punishment and guilt." And so we despised God's ordinances such as Baptism as though they were no good for anything, whereas making a pilgrimage to Rome was supposed to aid me. And then the pope confirmed this error in order to be ruler of the world and to possess the treasures of the world. Christ calls him the abomination of desolation (Matthew 24:15). "But I," says the Lord Christ, "am your Lord and your Savior. I died for you. Yet I will leave behind and give you a sign in which you may see and hear Me. Do not seek Me in heaven, at Rome, Compostela, or in a convent or monastery. I will come to you." Where? In a building out in the open, where people baptize and the Supper is received. There you can hear and see the signs; that is the work in which you should persevere. You will not have it better in Rome or a monastery. Indeed, you would even despise the signs of the Lord Christ if you were in those places. But they say, "Yet we are all baptized! Baptism is a plain and common thing." Guard yourself against that; for if it is a common, public thing, it is all the more valuable. The Lord Christ does not hide or conceal His treasures in private places or in a monastery, nor is the preaching office of God's Word carried out in private, but in the middle of town. Those are what we call God's signs. Therefore, if you run off to Compostela, you are making yourself special. Doing so will not make you better, as you suppose. Instead, stick to the signs which He has revealed to you. The Gospel will not deceive you nor will the signs. Let him who is a poor sinner hear the Absolution: "Your sins are forgiven you." However, the devil cannot tolerate this grace and mercy and has darkened and obscured these signs in many people. They claim it is something common, saying, "Am I to have no more

[8] All three of these were popular shrines of Mary. Here "Santiago" (and a few sentences later "Compostela") refers to Santiago de Compostela in Spain. On the practice of pilgrimages in the Reformation era, see Ernst Walter Zeeden, *Faith and Act: The Survival of Medieval Ceremonies in the Lutheran Reformation* (St. Louis: Concordia, 2012), pp. 66–70; Sara Warneke, "Pilgrimages," *OER* 3:272–74.

than the common people?" Now, Christ is not a helper of certain individuals, but a Savior of all people, so let us cling to and depend on Him alone.

Now learn carefully to distinguish between the institutions of God and of men. The pope has his institutions. The Lord Christ's institutions are preaching of the Gospel, Baptism, and the Supper. In these three things He wishes to speak with us and work in us. Thus we do nothing here. It is not our works, but God's Word and work. He who baptizes does not baptize of his own accord. The Baptism is not his work. He only lends his hand and tongue to it. The work that is done here is God's own true work, His alone. But since He desired that there should be a sign for us to see and perceive with our five senses, even though He is not really seen, He uses the hands of men for His witnesses. Thus the priest lends his mouth and tongue to the preaching office, and yet it is still God's Word, work, and institution. Go baptize your pig, if it is your word and your work! But what you should say is: "The word that I speak and the Baptism that I administer I do not do of my own accord, but I only lend my hand to them; for it is the Father, Son, and Holy Spirit who baptizes. Yet I devote my hand to the work so that it may be seen." So God has always given a sign to the God-fearing since the beginning of the world. As the psalm [60:4] says, "You have given a sign to those who fear You," which they might put up as a banner, that it might be open and common.

Therefore, whenever the three signs are not recognized, the situation is as it was in the papacy. One person thinks: "I do not want to go to church. They preach a great deal, but the people do not get any better. If it were God's Word, the people would get better. But I pray that God would enlighten me."—But such people despise these common signs and want God to do something special and peculiar for them, even though He has prepared signs of mercy and grace for you. You know this, yet you long for other signs! This is what people do. We want to have something special and to tie God to a secret place[9] and command. This is how it is with all who lose the glory of Baptism—they start looking for other such works, which in turn has given rise to all the sects, all of which crept into a secret place and asked God to give them a sign that He is gracious and merciful and will be won over by our holiness and devotion. But Christ warned us against this, saying, "They will say, 'He is in the inner chambers,' but do not go out" (Matthew 24:26). But this is all the result of people despising these signs, which were in fact signs of divine institution and given to us who were condemned and lost through Adam's fall, that we might cling to them. But if you try to look for them in the wilderness or in a monastery, you will not find them, for He has not located Himself there nor put any sign there. You will find the devil

[9] *Winkel*, or "corner."

there instead. But come to this sign which God has established, where He preaches the Gospel to us and strengthens us with the bread on the altar and with Baptism. And the Lord Christ will say, "You will see Me present bodily in My preaching, baptizing, and absolving, and distributing the Supper." Then we can say with certainty: "Here is God."—"But I do not see it!"—"Still, it is enough that it is visible and that He speaks with you in the mystery of Baptism, the Supper, and Absolution."—"But the holy angels appear to the sectarian spirits and speak with them"; likewise: "The apostles and Mary appear to the monks in monasteries!"—All this I will grant, for it serves to confirm their "order"; it is not Mary who appears to them, but Lucifer and his wretched angels. God will not strike His own mouth and call Himself a liar. Therefore, with their visions and revelations they have confirmed their blasphemy; however, I want none of this revelation. They immediately think it is an angel, but it is the devil. I say, "Saints Peter and Mary, stay up in heaven! I do not want your revelation in these matters of salvation where people's deliverance from sin and death is concerned. I want no revelation here, not even from all the angels, but I will say it is all a lie. I have my own revelation and epiphany: I have seen God's hand and mouth and His bodily food in which He has given me His body and blood. God appears to me through His Word; likewise, I lay hold of Him in Baptism; again, God appears to me through my schoolmaster, my parents, my preachers, and His Word; and again in the Absolution, when He says, "Your sins are forgiven you." Therefore, I do not ask for Moses or Elijah, St. Paul or Gabriel, for all these are still servants, even if their appearance was the most beautiful of all. Rather, I have the Lord Himself speaking to me. Is it not enough that He Himself has instituted the Word, Baptism, the Supper, and the Absolution? The devil appeared to St. Martin in the persona of Christ and said, "Your prayer has been heard. Be of good cheer!" For he suddenly took on the form of an angel, as may be seen in the evangelist Matthew, where you think you are only seeing an angel. But what did St. Martin do? At first he was troubled, for the devil used God's name. But he said, "No, Christ did not say that He would come with a royal crown." Poof! The Christ disguise instantly vanished.[10] Others must not have been aware of this method for recognizing and driving away the devil.

[10] The story is in Jacobus de Voragine (ca. 1230–ca. 1298), *The Golden Legend: Readings on the Saints*, trans. William Granger Ryan (Princeton, NJ: Princeton University Press, 2012), p. 684 (no. 166). There, the devil appeared in the form of Christ, wearing purple and a golden crown. St. Martin of Tours (ca. 336–397), instructed by the Holy Spirit, refused to believe that it was really Christ unless he saw the signs of Christ's Passion: the stigmata of the cross.

Now, then, as regards healing the fall which we suffered in Paradise, God has revealed to you a satisfaction[11] which was to apply to all men. Value it highly in your heart, and thank God the Father of all mercy for it, for He shows every kindness and gives us His Word, and then Baptism, which He instituted. Here I can say, "I have Your sign in the preaching office. It is not a man that I hear, but You." Likewise, in the Sacrament of the Altar He gives us His body and blood. (But if you go to Compostela, you will see wax signs, where the devil has provided help in the name of St. James.) For this reason they also are called signs of God—not mere, everyday signs as the Anabaptists reckon them. For God willed to come to you bodily and to dress you with His own holy suffering, so that when you are baptized, and then go to the Lord's Supper, hear the preaching, and receive the Absolution, you always think to yourself: "I do not hear a man." Put the baptizer, preacher, and minister of the Sacrament of the Altar out of sight. Likewise, if your parents rebuke you and repeat to you God's Word, you are not listening to them but to God's Word, so receive it the same way. Likewise, when a brother comforts you in your sadness, think to yourself that you are hearing God.[12] Other commands are properly the commands of a father, such as when he tells his son to go into the field. But when it concerns God's Word, what a father says is God's commandment.

From this discussion of the sacraments you should know that the sacraments are a divine institution and not instituted by men, and you need not have any question about the signs. If you eagerly desire a revelation from Christ, God, and the angels, you do not need it, for you have a revelation from heaven in Baptism—likewise, in preaching and in the Supper—and there is no need for God to reveal Himself to us in a special manner. Therefore, say, "I will stick to His common revelation of the Word and the work of Christ."

Second Sermon on Holy Baptism, on the Third Sunday after Epiphany January 27, 1538

Heretics[13] and deceivers will come along after us, so in order to maintain the right understanding of Baptism, it is our intention to preach on that subject

[11] *Gnugthuung*, i.e., "doing enough."

[12] Cf. *Smalcald Articles* (1537) III IV (Kolb-Wengert, p. 319; *Concordia*, p. 278).

[13] Translated by Matthew Carver from Martin Luther, *Dr. Martin Luther's Sämmtliche Werke*, 2nd series, vol. 20, part 1, ed. Ernst Ludwig Enders (Frankfurt am Main: Heyder & Zimmer, 1880), pp. 29–37. Cf. the stenographic notes for this sermon in WA 46:151–55 (Aland Pr 1694).

again. (Nevertheless, Baptism held up fairly well among the abominations of the papacy, since people were still being brought to Baptism.)

First of all, it is necessary in all sacraments to determine whether they are God's work and institution. For this reason, no one should take offense at the person who administers and distributes the Supper. It would be meet and right for those who administer the sacraments to believe and be righteous, but if he is secretly ungodly, we cannot therefore declare that the Baptism is not real.[14] We must be aware that Baptism is not the work of the man who gives it, but that God is using his hand to do it. And we who handle the sacraments are certainly supposed to be pure, but if that is not the case, it in no way subtracts from nor adds to Baptism.

There was a notable heresy held by the *Donatists*, who taught that when an ungodly servant of the Word distributed the sacraments, Baptism and the Supper were not real, since it says in Sirach [34:4]: "When a man is unclean, what can he make clean?" If a servant girl takes a handful of yeast, she will not make a veil clean. So it was, they thought, with Baptism. If the preacher is impure, the Baptism must also be nothing. And these Donatists played the game with the Catabaptists,[15] just as the Anabaptists do today, and the people flocked to them everywhere. But the sacraments are not a servant girl's dough or soot. Baptism is a precious washing, but you are using the example of human works and trying to compare them to divine works. Therefore, say, "God has clean fingers and hands; they cannot be defiled by my uncleanness." The sun is clean, too, but it often sheds light and shines on filth and unclean things, including thieves on the gallows and dead bodies, yet the sun is still clean. Much more does Baptism remain clean here, since it is God the Father Himself who baptizes. A defiled hand can do no harm to it.

It was a significant question, and one which was of great concern to all Christians, before it was made clear that Baptism is the work of God and not of any man. Do not look at who is baptizing. He may be righteous and holy personally, but with his own holiness he neither adds anything to Baptism nor takes anything away from it. Here you must not focus on who is standing there baptizing, but on what he is doing and what is happening. He does not stain and defile Baptism by his wickedness, nor does he sanctify or improve Baptism by his righteousness.

If I were baptized by St. Peter and someone else were baptized by Judas, as no doubt happened, then, although Judas is a scoundrel and St. Peter is a righteous apostle of Christ, yet Judas does not therefore make the Baptism

---

[14] *recht*, or "valid, right, legitimate."

[15] I.e., people who opposed Baptism, who claimed that the Baptism of the majority Catholic Church was invalid. Cf. G. W. H. Lampe, *A Patristic Greek Lexicon* (Oxford: Clarendon Press, 1961), s.v. "καταβαπτιστής."

bad. Likewise, the fact that St. Peter is a saint applies only to himself personally and in no way helps or applies to Baptism. On the other hand, the fact that Judas is Christ's betrayer does not hurt the Baptism which others received from him. The Donatists, however, said that Judas is ungodly, therefore his Baptism is not real either. Yet St. Augustine says, "Christ retained Baptism for Himself, that we might know that the minister's ungodliness is not detrimental to the Sacrament."

You have an excellent picture of this in the world. How often a prince has an unjust officer and attendant! How often a lady has a wicked, unfaithful servant in her house or a maidservant who is a prostitute! Yet the prince says to his officer: "Give this to so-and-so," and the gift is not therefore rendered bad or evil by the attendant or maidservant, but it comes from their master, and an unjust, ungodly officer does not defile his master's gift and present, nor does a righteous officer add anything to it. The gift is neither impaired nor improved. Therefore, it is a heresy to despise and reject Baptism on the basis of persons.

And Anabaptists similarly say, "The child did not believe when he was baptized, so his Baptism is not real, and he has to be baptized again when he matures."—Now suppose that it is true (which it is not) that Baptism is weakened by unbelievers, and an old man comes and asks to be baptized and yet is ungodly, and nevertheless desires Baptism because of his sins. I ask, is that Baptism real and true? The old man does not believe but makes a mockery of it, and is looking only for money to be given to him as a gift from his godparents. To this reply: "Let the nature of the person who gives or receives Baptism be free; whether he be called a Peter or a Judas, it does nothing for Baptism nor does it help it, for it is a divine Baptism and work." So the fact that you do not believe is your own fault; nor is it false when a Jew is baptized. Just as when a prince and lord gives away a field or castle it is no fiction, but the thing in itself, so Baptism is real and true in itself, and God, who gives it, is also true. And if you are given a present and you accept it, and, though it is gold, you do not believe that it is a real and good present or gold, it is not therefore transformed into earth or mud by your disbelief. Likewise, whether the messenger boy is righteous or wicked, the gift is good. And no matter whether you are wicked or righteous, or refuse to believe that it is gold, it is still gold and will continue to be so.

It is necessary to press and preach this diligently because of the Anabaptists, who claim that children do not have faith. Yet were we to suppose that they do not have faith, nevertheless they ought to be baptized. For if a Jew who was baptized reconverts a year later and says, "I was not serious about that Baptism. Please help and advise me!"—should he be rebaptized? No, let him cling to the Baptism that was given to him before.

In our long lives we have often committed many sins. Are we always to be rebaptized after we sin? Even if you do not have faith now, you may have faith at some future time. When a prince sends out a decree for a thief to be hanged, and certain people disobey and do not carry out the edict or decree, I ask, is the disobedience of those who rebel against this command so strong and powerful that they could cancel or abolish the edict or command? Neither in truth can I, by my wickedness, nullify the commands of God. If I told my parents: "I will not obey you anymore," do you think that the Fourth Commandment would therefore cease to be valid? Would a father therefore cease to be a father? Or the prince cease to be prince? Quite the opposite! The commandment is all the stronger for your disobedience, and God will condemn you forever. In the same way, if you do not believe, though you are baptized, woe to you! It is to your eternal damnation. If in your unbelief you wished to renounce it, would you not be justly condemned? It does not logically follow to say, "I have misused the name of God; therefore, the Second Commandment is no longer valid." Rather, because you have blasphemed and dishonored the name of God, you will be punished as a blasphemer. So, too, if Baptism is no different from a goose bath (as the Anabaptists blasphemously claim), it does no harm. But because God is true and that Baptism was founded and instituted by the true God, it will be harmful to you.

We see this error before our eyes, yet these people cannot be convinced, but say, "If the faith is not genuine, then the Baptism is not real." But just you turn it around and say, "If the Baptism is not real, then the faith is not genuine." It is the same in the papacy with those who have gone into monasteries. Thus the Anabaptists act wrongly and wickedly, even if they maintain both suppositions: that those who administered Baptism were evil and those who received Baptism were also unbelieving and wicked. For God's command is God's edict, no matter whether it be a townsman or a peasant who is concerned, or whether he obeys or disobeys God's command. Otherwise authorities and all estates would be uprooted the moment anyone says, "I will not obey you; therefore, the command of God counts for nothing." No, you will see in due time what you have done. You cannot negate Baptism, but God can still punish you. They neither see nor hear that Baptism is not a work of men and that it depends not on my faith, who receives Baptism, nor on the faith of the preacher who administers and gives it, but on the strength and truth of God.

Accordingly, if you wish to benefit from Baptism, it is right for you to have faith. Then you have the power of Baptism, which washes away our sins and bestows on us forgiveness of sins and pulls us out of death and gives us eternal life. Therefore, regardless of what kind of people we are, both he who confers Baptism and the other who receives it are handling the work of

God. If he who gives it is righteous, well then; but if he who receives it is evil, for him it is evil. However, if you rebaptize, it is as if the first Baptism were nothing. Therefore, you make God a liar and say that that work of God is nothing and false. It is frightening to hear people blaspheming the work of God, saying, "What is wrong is that he who receives Baptism has no faith, so the Baptism is worthless." Yet if someone were awarded a hundred guilders[16] and he refused to take it, would the hundred guilders not retain their value? His refusal of the money has no negative effect on the gold. So it is with Baptism also.

If you question an Anabaptist on this point, he will say, "Both he who gives the Baptism and he who receives it must believe." How do you know? "Well," he replies, "the person being baptized is asked if he believes. Then he says, 'Yes.' On the basis of this affirmation, he is baptized." Yet you still do not know for sure whether he believes. What, then, are we to do in this case? Shall I not baptize until I am certain of the faith of him who is receiving Baptism? Then I cannot know if anyone's word is true. Thus it is impossible for me ever to baptize someone on the basis of his own words, since I cannot see into anyone's heart. Yet I hear that both are supposed to have faith; but I do not see it and cannot see it. Therefore, they have more error in their administration of Baptism than they attribute to us with their blasphemy and slander. In their system, I would be unable to absolve anyone in confession nor give him the Supper, if it depended on faith. I simply say, "If you believe and are baptized, you will be saved," and do not inquire whether you truly believe or not. Since you have asked me for Baptism, I give it to you, commending you to God and leaving you to see to your own faith. In this way, he who gives the Baptism is safe and is not bound to whether he who receives the Baptism believes or not. Rather, he has the command: "Go into all the world and teach the Gospel to all nations, baptizing them," etc. [Mark 16:15; Matt. 28:19]. So whoever receives Baptism and believes has the benefit and fruit of Baptism, but whoever does not believe still has the real Baptism, no matter what kind of person gives it.

This is not a new error, then, but also existed in the time of Augustine. And the Papists have become more furious, impudent, and wicked since they heard that the wickedness of the person who gives a Baptism in no way hurts Baptism. But they should watch out. All the sacrifices of God remain undefiled, no matter whether the priest's wickedness is present or not.

If this point is maintained, do not let rebaptism attack you, for you can say to the Anabaptists: "You are making God's work dependent on human

[16] *hundert Gulden.* A hundred guilders was a very large, though not astronomical, sum for ordinary people. See AE 57:143 n. 14; 68:40 n. 61; cf. above, p. 16 n. 7.

character."[17] Know first of all that Baptism is the work of God and was instituted and founded by God. I could also speak here of what the pope has washed away from Baptism, but that has been frequently discussed elsewhere.[18] So because Baptism is not a work of man but a divine institution, you see where the power of Baptism comes from. It is not a bather's bath or the bath of a mother washing her child, but a divine work; and therefore Baptism has divine power. This presents us with the true understanding of Baptism so that we do not discount it.

First, when all things were created and the water was as yet without fish, God said, "Let the waters stir" [Gen. 1:20]. Then all the waters were filled with fish, and where there had been no fish there were fish, not by nature but by the Word of God, when God said, "Let the waters stir with fish." Thus from the power of the Word, all the waters had fish, even when no one had put fish into them. They might well say that ducks cause fish to fall into ponds, but here there is nothing except for this Word of God. When God said, "Let the waters stir with fish," all the fish appeared. What else should He not be able to do then? When He says of Baptism: "In this water I will wash away and forgive sins," and when a preacher says, "Be clean from all sins," then it is no longer the water which a cook in a house uses. Just as, when God says, "Let the waters stir," it is no longer the former water but is now filled with fish, so also Baptism—while it is water before the Word of God is added to it, and a common water of which a cow might drink or which a cook might use for boiling and washing—when the Word of God is spoken over it and Baptism is administered in the name of the Father and of the Son and of the Holy Spirit, then it has the efficacy and power to wash away sin and deliver from death. So, too, what would Adam and Eve have done without the addition of God's Word: "Increase and multiply," etc. [Gen. 1:28]? The Word makes them fruitful and puts milk in the mother's breasts. In this way, Baptism must not be regarded as mere, ordinary water, which is precisely how the Anabaptists regard it, nor as the pope has foolishly treated this Sacrament, as we shall discuss next week.

---

[17] *auf Menschen Person*, or "on the personal characteristics of human beings."

[18] See *Babylonian Captivity* (1520), AE 36:57–81.

Third Sermon on Holy Baptism, on the Fifth Sunday after Epiphany February 10, 1538

In[19] order that the Sacrament of Holy Baptism may remain familiar to us Christians, especially to young people who are growing up from day to day, let us preach about it a little while longer. For the fact that Baptism is not treated diligently comes from the fact that the pope himself did not understand what Baptism is. In addition, there is still before our eyes the error of the Anabaptists, who dishonor and slander Baptism. Therefore, we must preach about it diligently for ourselves and our descendants and draw attention to three things: first, the institution of Baptism; second, what it is in itself; and, third, what power it has.

First, Baptism is no human invention or institution, but it is the institution of God. If the Anabaptists believed this, they would not have called it a dog's bath. And the devil himself speaks the same way of Baptism, for he sees the water only with the eyes of a cow or as a cow looks at a new gate.[20] For he does not regard who instituted or ordained it, for if they would consider the fact that it is God's ordinance, they would have a high regard for Baptism. But because they regard it as a human addition and statute, Baptism is nothing in their eyes. But if it were consecrated water,[21] of which God knows nothing, then you might well despise it; but the teaching of the Gospel shows that Christ Himself says, "Go and teach all nations, baptizing them" [Matt. 28:19].

Second, it is necessary to know what Baptism is in itself, of what sort it is. There stands the text, as Christ says, "Go, baptizing" [Matt. 28:19]. And in John 3 [:5] it says that if a man is not born again by water and the Holy Spirit, he cannot enter the kingdom of heaven. Again: St. John says, "There are three things which bear record on earth: the Spirit, water, and blood" [1 John 5:7–8]. And St. Paul calls it "a washing of rebirth" [Titus 3:5] which God "has purified" (Ephesians 5 [:26]).

These and other verses clearly show that Baptism in its essence is two things: both the washing with water and the Word together. Therefore, if you are asked about Baptism, say, "It encompasses two things: first, the water which is poured, then the Word." First of all, God is the Founder, and He

---

[19] Translated by Matthew Carver from Martin Luther, *Ungedruckte Predigten D. Martin Luthers aus den Jahren 1537–1540*, ed. Georg Buchwald (Leipzig: G. Strübigs Verlag, 1905), pp. 283–89. Cf. the stenographic notes for this sermon in WA 46:167–73 (Aland Pr 1697).

[20] The saying indicates thoughtless astonishment at something new and is explained in Wander 1:100, "ansehen" no. 37.

[21] *Weihwasser*, commonly called "holy water" in modern Roman Catholic parlance.

wants His work and His Word to be named and kept. Now, as the Anabaptists reject the *Founder*, others remove the *Word of God* from sight and look only at the water, and then say, "The water is nothing unless you believe!" And therefore they base Baptism on our own worthiness. Yet do not by any means separate the water and the Word. In Baptism, the Word is: "In the name of the Father and of the Son and of the Holy Spirit" [Matt. 28:19].

This Word of God makes Baptism, and without this Word, Baptism is nothing; and thus Baptism does not depend on our faith. For even in the papacy they did not have this understanding. Therefore, I earnestly and diligently press this point, that preachers may know that Baptism in its essence is water and the Word of God, when the preacher says, "I baptize you in the name of the Father and of the Son and of the Holy Spirit." And women ought to learn these words, that in time of need they may administer emergency Baptism. Now, the word in this passage seems trivial, and the water has a poor appearance. Yet do not let that mislead you, but look at Him who commanded that Baptism be done. For He only says a word, such as: "Waters, stir!" [Gen. 1:20], and instantly by this word all the ponds and rivers are full of fish. This is God's institution and power, and Augustine says of this: "Baptism touches the body and washes the soul."[22] How does this happen? Here the Dominicans, Thomas [Aquinas], and others argue that in the water there is a secret, divine power which the Holy Spirit has inserted into it, and this is what washes and purifies the soul.[23] This is an obscure way of speaking. He saw the smoke but did not know where the fire was. What use are obscure terms, since we have more certain knowledge? Therefore, say that here there is water and God's Word, and for that reason it has the power to cleanse the soul from sins. Later, [Duns] Scotus disputed this and said that we should not think or imagine that the power is in the water, but the power of Baptism comes from the fact that God Himself is present in it and wishes to baptize by the Holy Spirit.[24] They saw that it had to be something more than the water. I could certainly interpret it as saying that the secret power is God's Word. But the words and opinions of others are strange and

---

[22] Augustine, *On the Gospel of St. John*, tractate 80.3: "And whence has water so great an efficacy, as in touching the body to cleanse the soul, save by the operation of the word; and that not because it is uttered, but because it is believed? For even in the word itself the passing sound is one thing, the abiding efficacy another" (NPNF[1] 7:344; cf. PL 35:1840).

[23] Cf. Thomas Aquinas, *ST*, 3. q. 62 art. 4 (Blackfriars 56:60–65).

[24] John Duns Scotus (ca. 1265–1308), *In Tertivm Et Qvartvm Sententiarvm Qvaestiones Svbtilissimae* (Antverpiae: apud Ioannem Keerbergivm, 1620), part 4, dist. 1, qq. 4–5, pp. 21–27. Question 4 (p. 21) deals with "whether it is possible that any sacrament that is in any way perfect may have active causality with respect to conferring grace," where he quotes the same passage from Augustine's commentary on John (see above, n. 22). In q. 5 (pp. 22–27), he refutes Thomas Aquinas' position.

obscure, and I cite them here so that you may not resort to their language. Having rejected this, then, say, "Baptism is a washing with water along with the divine Word, with which I wash and pour the water over, or dip into the water, and add to it these words: 'I baptize you in the name of the Father and of the Son and of the Holy Spirit.'" In the same way, in the Sacrament [of the Altar] there is bread and wine, if it is in any sense to be real eating and drinking, and the institution must be added, which is that Christ says, "The bread is My body, and the cup is My blood"; likewise: "This do in remembrance of Me!" [cf. Luke 22:19; 1 Cor. 11:24–25]. Now, if you have God's Word here, it is all-powerful, and then the water baptizes the soul and washes it in such a way that it is cleansed from all sins and from death. At this point a man is born again. Here the Word has this power. For the Father, Son, and Holy Spirit are baptizing me. Just think whether they might have some power or other, that sin might be washed away! If not, then cast Baptism away! But if they have divine power and authority, why do you not listen to God's Word? Thus Baptism is a "washing of rebirth and renewal" [Titus 3:5] so that it makes a new man.

Long ago, when pagans and Christians were mixed together, this was the distinction: When Christians were baptized, they dressed in a white robe and wore it for a week; infant Baptism was not yet common at that time. And this week they referred to as the "white week" and "White Sunday." Their practice of going about dressed this way may have been a reaction to the Jews, perhaps as a distinction for those who were baptized, that it might be known that they had been washed and cleansed not with plain water but by Baptism. When there is a Baptism now, the white robe has disappeared, and only the baptismal gown remains. The baptismal font is also small today, since the infants who are baptized are small. By this ceremony they show that the washing of Baptism is not a plain bath but God's bath in which He Himself baptizes—Father, Son, and Holy Spirit. Because God's Word is in Baptism, we cannot attribute power to Baptism enough. Here God washes not the outside only, but the whole man, so that it is a "washing of renewal and rebirth" [Titus 3:5], and the one baptized becomes a new man who goes about in an angelic garment and by Baptism enters the state of innocence.

Accordingly, if you first believe that Baptism is God's institution, you will not hold it equal to the pope's banners, candles, consecrated water, and censers. Distinguish them from each other as heaven is distinguished from earth. For the Turk and the Jews still have a great deal of washing, baptizing, and cleansing in the present day. But it is all as if someone were washing a dirty sheet. But what is the use of their washing in this way and the pope having his consecrated water? Here I can say that the Turk's baptism and washing is a dog's bath, for it does not have the support of the Founder.

Second, it has neither God's Word nor God's power and working. Even if St. Peter or St. John ordered you to wash yourself, if it does not have as its support: "I, the Father, Son, and Holy Spirit, baptize you," your washing and baptism is nothing. St. Paul would not tolerate it when they boasted: "I am of Cephas; another, of Apollo" (1 Corinthians 1 [:12]). For those who had been taught and baptized by St. Peter wanted to be most important. Then he said, "Were you baptized into my name, or did I die for you? I thank God that I baptized no one" [cf. 1 Cor. 1:13–14]. It is not "Baptized in the name of Peter," but "in the name of Christ" or "in the name of God." This is how we stand against the Anabaptists and all the obscure language of the papacy. Thus Baptism was consistently done in the name of the Father and of the Son and of the Holy Spirit; and even if it was not understood, yet they used the Word and water, and so they were truly baptized. Even if Baptism were given by pagans, they were nevertheless truly baptized.

St. Augustine writes of two, one a Christian, the other a pagan, who both baptized other people. Then the pagan asked whether the Christian preacher's Baptism were better than his. Augustine answered: "Baptism is not founded on my holiness and wickedness, for it goes 'baptized in the name of the Father and of the Son and of the Holy Spirit,' not 'in the name of the preacher.'" Therefore, Baptism is water with the Word of God, even if it were done in such a way that one person baptized the other in an emergency, and one was not a Christian but wanted to be, and nevertheless both believed that it was a true Baptism, the one would receive not only the true Baptism but also its working and power.

In the ceremonies of the papacy, people did not have God's Word, and we keep admonishing that we certainly ought to have God's Word before us, and that all that we do is instituted by God and that God's Word is present. If we were to lie on our knees for our whole life, we would be unable to thank God sufficiently for revealing to us by His Word that Baptism is pleasing to Him. We should also know that included in God's Word is the estate of parents and authorities. Such a life is pleasing to God. But the devil casts away this revealed will of God and replaces it with something else. In the papacy, we thought that we had lost Baptism.[25] Therefore, we entered monasteries, went on pilgrimages, and purchased indulgences, but we were like the foolish virgins in the Gospel who had no oil in their lamps, that is, were without faith [Matt. 25:1–13]. For we let go of what God commanded and directed and what pleases Him, and instead laid hold of what pleases ourselves, saying, "I have a good intention."[26] May the executioner strike!

---

[25] See below, on Jerome's "plank," pp. 77–78.

[26] "Reason judges this way about all the doctrines of the faith; for it does not understand that the supreme form of worship is to hear the voice of God and to believe, but it supposes

We have enough good works to do that we may remain with what God has given us and revealed to us as His will. We have Baptism, the Supper, the Absolution, and the preaching of the Gospel, as well as the Lord's Prayer, and are overflowing with heavenly wisdom and great understanding of spiritual goods. But the devil continually tears us away from them. The Jews could not remain in their temple, but ran to the beautiful meadows under the linden trees and oak trees, and up the high mountains, and built altars there, intending thereby to worship God. He is continually taking away that with which God has revealed Himself, such as at the Jordan on the day of the Epiphany, when the Lord revealed Himself and made Himself visible: the Father in the voice, when He said, "This is My beloved Son in whom I am well pleased; to Him shall you listen" [Matt. 17:5]; the Son standing in His human nature and submitting to Baptism; and the Holy Spirit appearing in the form of a dove [Matt. 3:16]. Thus the Godhead made itself known in the Baptism of Christ. Therefore, whoever does here what God commands, pleases God well, and he obtains salvation. For He says, "Whoever believes and is baptized will be saved" [Mark 16:16].

Is this not a glorious sun and great revelation of the divine will? Yet we do not look at it, do not pay attention to it, but the pope says, "Take up the cowl, say Mass, go on a pilgrimage!" which is only a human invention and idea, and the divine Majesty is despised, and what He commanded is neglected, and what He did not call for, but rather forbade, is sought after. Therefore, God should send not only the Turk upon us but also the devil.

In addition, these things were aided by the dangerous saying of St. Jerome, which they vigorously adopt, that penance is another plank after shipwreck. Shipwreck means someone was in a state of salvation, but after Baptism falls back into sin, and the Baptism is lost and no longer counts as anything. This makes it necessary to think of another board or plank to take hold of by which we may swim ashore. This, then, is the penance of my own works. The way in which St. Jerome intended it I leave aside;[27] I only show this so that it may be seen how dangerous it is to speak of something with alien and unfamiliar words. There can be no better and safer way of speaking than with divine words. The misuse arose from the fact that the pope preached in this way: if a boy of seven years turns bad and then falls into sin, he no longer has Baptism's power and working and is therefore directed to his own works. This resulted in the whole world being filled with monks, nuns, and priests, and the papacy inventing the idea that after committing sins people must help and aid themselves. This led to all

that what it chooses on its own and what it does with a so-called good intention and from its own devotion is pleasing to God" (Luther, *Lectures on Galatians* [1531], AE 26:228).

[27] See above, "To the Christian Reader," pp. viii–x.

the pilgrimages, purgatory, and other forms of service to God. It is preached even today in the papacy, when they say that Baptism only takes away the original sin which is innate in us, but those who have matured and grown up can make satisfaction for their sin and disobedience, and God will then say to them: "Because you do so many good works, you shall have forgiveness of your sins." This is the pope's doctrine. On this basis were founded the canonical rules,[28] monastic works, and altars. But know, in opposition to this, that Baptism, once given, is an eternal covenant. If I receive Baptism before I believe, as I have said of a Jew who was baptized and afterward said, "Now I repent,"[29] he should not be rebaptized, for his Baptism is genuine and true, even if it does not bear fruit in him. So also, if I sin after Baptism, the Baptism remains, but it is of no benefit to me. [If] I have fallen into murder by unbelief, then I have lost the use and benefit of Baptism, even though the Baptism remains. But if I say, "God, be merciful to me, a sinner!" and receive Absolution for my sins, then I return to the benefit of Baptism and say, "I believe in Jesus Christ and wish to die in Baptism." Although I have acted against Baptism, Christ will forgive me.

For this reason, monks are worse than Anabaptists, for they have taught the following: In the event that someone sins after Baptism, if he enters a monastery, he obtains renewal. Likewise: once they have made a vow to join an order, they are as clean from sins as if they had just come from Baptism.[30] Then, if I should regret that I have become a monk, the renewal is lost; but if it is my earnest intent that, were I not already a monk, I would wish to be one, I would have the fruit and benefit of the order once again. Those are truly Anabaptists.

All this makes us regard Baptism as something useless. But know that in Baptism we are adorned and cleansed by the blood of Christ. If I remain in Baptism, I hear: "Whoever believes and is baptized shall be saved" [Mark 16:16]; but if I fall into sin, I turn back and cling to Baptism and say, "The Lord Christ alone has washed me with His blood." For this reason, Baptism is an eternal covenant. For whoever receives it has this condition: that he will remain in it and fight against sin and the devil. Accordingly, when we fall out of Baptism, God helps us back into it. For it remains firm so that we do not drown at sea. Thus no satisfaction is imposed on us either before or after Baptism. He alone is the Lamb of God that was slain from the beginning of the world [Rev. 13:8]. His satisfaction therefore avails us from the beginning of our life even to our death. In this way, the right understanding

---

[28] *Canonica*

[29] See above, pp. 69–70.

[30] See above, p. 47.

of Baptism could be maintained by saying that we cannot make amends[31] for sin after shipwreck. For it is from this that all the abominations of the Mass and processions and invocation of saints proceed. For they thought that if someone sinned after Baptism, he had to make amends for sin.

Nevertheless, contrary to the pope's preaching, God sustained the practice of holding the image of the crucified Christ before one who was dying and having him say, "I believe in Him!" Likewise, the Word of God remained in preaching and Baptism. This was very right, and it was sustained by God alone. Otherwise it would have been impossible in the vast multitude of idolatries and superstitions. And to evildoers who were condemned, they promised: "You have deserved death in the sight of the world, for which be sorry! But it does not help your soul." But others taught to the contrary that, if those who were on their deathbed put on a cowl, they obtained the forgiveness of sins. Likewise, they said, "We will give you all our good works." Bah! Give them to the devil! Those are scoundrels who have broken all divine works in pieces. God sustained only this comfort for the dying. Therefore, they said, "Far more souls fly to heaven from the gallows than from the graveyard." But in my opinion, it was the devil who said it. It would be true, perhaps, if a proper preacher were there at the gallows with the dying and showed them the benefit of Baptism. But when people are pointed to the graveyard and told to trust in their good works, say, "My making satisfaction is useless. Before the world I will gladly make satisfaction, but before God, my satisfaction before and after Baptism is the innocent blood of Christ, the fact that He shed His innocent blood for me. He was wounded for our iniquities" [Isa. 53:5].

Therefore, we should make sure that we always retain Baptism, and even if we sometimes lose its use, we should make sure that we take hold of it again. Now, if you understand this as the plank on which you can swim back to the ship, it is not bad. But if you relate the plank to good works, it is bad. Thus up till now we have dealt with the second point of Baptism.

---

[31] *büßen*, or "do penance."

Fourth Sermon on Holy Baptism, on the Sixth Sunday after Epiphany February 17, 1538

The[32] first thing that we heard about Baptism is that it is not a work or invention of man, as is the Mass,[33] but an institution or established ordinance from heaven by God. We should be careful to observe this fact so that this sacrament may retain its due honor. Nicodemus was told: "What is born of flesh is flesh" [John 3:6]. For this reason, what has been instituted in the papacy are all fleshly ideas. They have a fine appearance and gleam with grandeur, so that even Baptism seems far less important than such human statutes and ordinances. Therefore, we should observe the glory and majesty of Baptism.

Second, we heard what Baptism is in its essence—namely, water and God's Word together—so that when we dip the child into the Baptism and say, "I baptize you in the name of the Father and of the Son and of the Holy Spirit," it has a petty appearance. It seems far better to sing a sequence about St. Mary.[34] Baptism loses its beauty and majesty by being performed and administered by a man. But it does not depend on that, even though a man's hand is added. Nevertheless, Baptism is God's ordinance. If there were a hundred thousand priests and they were all wearing gold chasubles and had a church made of diamonds, that would be nothing compared to baptizing a child according to God's command. Baptism should be viewed in this way so that we may repel those blind leaders who regard it as plain water and put God's Word and command out of sight.

Third, we should see this Baptism as ordained by God not only in order to be God's Word and water but also to have a power and virtue by which one is justified, and not to be a mere spectacle for the eyes, as though, once the water has been poured over the child, all is complete, but to have the power

---

[32] Translated by Matthew Carver from Martin Luther, *Ungedruckte Predigten D. Martin Luthers aus den Jahren 1537–1540*, ed. Georg Buchwald (Leipzig: G. Strübigs Verlag, 1905), pp. 289–93. Cf. the stenographic notes for this sermon in WA 46:174–78 (Aland Pr 1698).

[33] Here "Mass" is being defined as the specific liturgy of the Mass with its false doctrine, as stipulated in the Roman Church. In the Augsburg Confession (1530) and its Apology (1531), "Mass" is defined differently, as the Lord's Supper in general, without a specific doctrine or liturgy connoted.

[34] I.e., a sequence hymn. These hymns usually had long, difficult melodies and profound texts. For examples, see "Christians to the Paschal Victim," *Lutheran Service Book* (St. Louis: Concordia, 2006), 460; "Zion, to Thy Savior Singing," *Evangelical Lutheran Hymnary* (St. Louis: MorningStar, 1996), 321; "Near the Cross Was Mary Weeping," *Evangelical Lutheran Hymnary* 294; "At the Cross, Her Station Keeping," *Lutheran Book of Worship* (Minneapolis: Augsburg, 1978), 110. A large collection of sequence hymns in English translation is in *The New Office Hymn Book*, part 1 (London: Novello & Co., 1908), nos. 116–50.

and ability to wash away sins and produce a new birth, taking a person from the old birth which he received from his parents and giving him rebirth unto eternal life, adorning him with innocence and eternal life. Who can describe this power by which a man, born in sin, has the glory of receiving in Baptism a fountain of youth[35] and being cleansed from his sins and grafted into eternal life? Washing away sin, removing God's wrath—these are divine works. The pope would also like to have attributed them to his own inventions, even as they have preached that whoever is obedient to the pope is in a state of salvation;[36] likewise, if they excommunicate someone, even if it is done unjustly, nevertheless people must be afraid of it. Likewise, the devil tried to make people newly born when they put on a monk's cowl, and thus attributed divine power to his foolish works. We went to Santiago and to St. Peter's in Rome, hoping they would deliver us from sins, when they were themselves children of destruction and nevertheless boasted with grandiose words that they would deliver people from sins. Suddenly people rushed into the cloister, though there was only corruption there. We may be very grateful to God that we have seen these abominations and been delivered from them.

Now then, the power of Baptism is that a human being is born again; that is, he is stripped of the old skin and old birth which he brings with him, such as sin and death, and puts on the true baptismal gown, that is, the innocence and death of Christ. Therefore, when you are baptized, remember that you are washed in a bath which is called the rebirth, and look to the Founder who ordained it.

Where does Baptism get this power? It is God's institution, and the Lord Christ, along with His death, suffering, bloodshed, and merits, is in Baptism. For when Christ is baptized, heaven opens above Him, and the Father's voice is heard, and the Holy Spirit is seen. Therefore, Baptism is a washing in which we are washed by the blood of the innocent Lamb, Christ. He pays for sin and puts death to death. This power and ability is not found in the pope's Mass, requiem,[37] or pilgrimages, but there is only one innocent Lamb who shed His blood and overcame death; and since it is not in the cowl and tonsure, it is to be sought in Baptism, in the Supper, the Gospel, and the Absolution. We are sure that all these things are instituted by God.

---

[35] *Jüngelbad,* or "washing of rejuvenation."

[36] According to the 1302 bull *Unam sanctam* promulgated by Pope Boniface VIII (r. 1294–1303) and reaffirmed by the Fifth Lateran Council in 1516: "It is altogether necessary to salvation for every human creature to be subject to the Roman pontiff." See Norman P. Tanner, ed., *Decrees of the Ecumenical Councils* (London: Sheed & Ward; Washington, DC: Georgetown University Press, 1990), 1:643–44.

[37] I.e., the Mass for the dead.

This is certain and is seasoned and anointed with the innocent blood of Christ. It has the Father, Son, and Holy Spirit with His ordinance and Word. It all comes from the merit of Christ. For this reason, the fathers said that all the sacraments flowed from the side of Christ. The blood of Christ flows into Baptism, into the chalice, and Absolution. This is aptly depicted, for the sense here is that His suffering earned forgiveness of sins, and He has it declared throughout the world that Baptism is to wash us from sins. This is why St. Paul, writing to Titus [3:5], refers to it as "a washing of rebirth" and says that it is a bath that was instituted for our washing, that we might be born again, as though from another mother, and made new. Thus Baptism has the whole Godhead in it, especially the Lord Christ, who cleanses us with His blood. So when we know that Baptism, by the blood of Christ, has such an effect on people that whoever is washed in it is cleansed by the blood of Christ, then there is truly forgiveness of sins and deliverance from death and bestowal of righteousness and eternal life.

This power of Baptism cannot be sufficiently treated as it deserves, but let us here follow the words of St. Paul, that everything flows from the merit of Christ. Keep well this fact that Baptism is Christ's institution.

Third, [by the power of Baptism] death is overcome, and we are given the true baptismal gown, which is innocence. Thus you are hearing abundantly what the godly ought to learn and know. We can in good conscience boast that we have taught you everything that God has revealed. You have the catechism, likewise the articles of the Christian faith.[38] You can pray, and you have many glorious exhortations to prayer. Likewise, you have rightly understood Baptism, the Supper, and the Absolution, and [you know] that our doctrine is the true Gospel and that you have been delivered from all the burdens of papistic confession, as well as of purgatory, pilgrimages, and invocation of saints, to which a great deal of money and possessions were devoted and by which body, soul, and property were sorely oppressed. If you keep these things, I can say with St. Paul that you lack nothing except to wait for the coming of the great God [Titus 2:13], and also that He would collect our body hereafter.

[Admonition]

It is therefore my hope that we are satisfying our office. Oh, that our life might follow accordingly![39] I eagerly wish that people would fast as they

---

[38] *des christlichen Glaubens*, or "the Christian creed."

[39] In the following section, Luther gives suggestions for fasting and self-discipline. This sermon was preached on the first Sunday of pre-Lent (*Septuagesima*). The thoughts and plans of the people were apparently turned toward the excesses of Carnival, followed by the remembrance or observance of fasting during Lent.

used to in the Christian Church long ago. In the papacy I saw no fasting either. In the time of Saints Augustine and Ambrose, they fasted on Saturday until evening. That would be an admirable and worthy custom. But this work belongs to the common man; my hand is too weak for it. Similarly, in the old days, whenever there was a plague or war, Christians gathered together and prayed, fasted, and listened to God's Word, in order to be delivered from calamity. This is the source of Rogation Week,[40] though it has become a disgrace. It was started long ago with good intentions, but it was perverted, and it resulted in the St. Mark's procession, which St. Gregory established because of a severe plague that occurred in his time. Similarly, Rogation Week came from heretics. I would like to advise in favor of [such fasting], if the temporal lords and rulers could manage to have people kept from excessive feasting and drinking, so that abstinence from eating meat were observed for one or two days a week. It is not a task for me, but it would be an excellent thing to be decreed by the princes, so that people might be made to abstain from meat a little. Otherwise it will get worse and worse. What need is there for people to live as though they were going to devour everything at once? It will end disgracefully. If it is begun soberly, it might well continue that way. Otherwise, if it came down from the pulpit, it would be turned into a service for God, and then one law after another would be passed until at last they would be made articles of faith, and then it would be neglected once more and turned into a hunting party and fishing frenzy. If our elector[41] will not look into the matter, I cannot do so for him. If it were possible, it would be good for us to abstain from meat two days, such as Friday and Saturday, or only once. In an evening, a monk in the monastery drank three flagons of beer, and at noon there was a very good meal, and on Fridays and Saturdays they at least had good fish to eat. I did not see any proper fasting except for what I did of my own accord and voluntarily, and as I said of St. Ambrose above, it would be admirable if such fasting were observed by Christendom and the people lived more moderately in the evening. For excessive eating and drinking leads to a dissolute and disorderly way of life, and in the process young people are brought up poorly. Furthermore, in the past there has been some lax behavior in the merriment of Shrove Tuesday, to the point where all kinds of mischief, unchastity, and other sad things have resulted.

---

[40] *die Kreuzwoche*, or "Cross Week." This was the three days after *Rogate* (the Fifth Sunday of Easter, the Sunday before Ascension), formerly celebrated with special Masses and processions in the open field.

[41] I.e., John Frederick (r. 1532–47).

But I implore the rector[42] and mayor to abolish the Carnival play,[43] for it is no longer likely to limit itself to joyful merriment, but is turning into vomiting and fighting. And if someone will not be satisfied with chaste merriment, he may justly be deprived of it. If you want to be a pig and go out all year and run around the city streets, I would like to submit my request that it be stopped. I do not want it resting on me. I have enough sin already and have no desire to bring upon myself the sins of others. Therefore, I exhort both the rector and the council not to paint the devil above the door.[44] I see that, under the guise of the Gospel, people are taking up a dissolute way of life. I hear that one person paid a price of nine guilders from his allowance for a pair of pants.[45] Your parents sent you here to learn godliness and good skills. In the old days, when boys were sent here, they were placed under the strict charge of the preceptors, and money was put not into their hands but into those of the preceptors. When students become their own masters and can do as they please, it is not a good sign. Then all good in Wittenberg is done for, and it will result in a Capernaum. Do not think it is no sin when you wear such fancy clothes. It is arrogant flaunting and a pointless waste of your father's inheritance. With that fashion, I would not want to be a preacher for an hour. God showers down upon us all manner of wisdom, and now townsman and peasant alike want to be wasteful and to cheat and swindle each other; no one cares about the poor nor the pastors in the villages nor the poor orphans. Thus I fear it will turn into a Sodom and Gomorrah. There, too, there was abundance of bread, so that they feasted and walked idly and were proud, and then committed sin. Therefore, those cities were razed to the ground. This is also happening now, and it is the sin of the Sodomites. Therefore, they fell into great sin with Lot. Earlier, they

[42] I.e., the rector of the University of Wittenberg.

[43] *Nachtspiel = Fastnachtspiel.* Shrovetide or Carnival dramas ridiculed the established authorities with costumed parodies of clergy and local leaders engaged in mock religious rituals, presided over by a king of fools. For the Carnival plays of Nürnberg's Hans Sachs, see Robert Aylett, trans. and ed., *Translations of the Carnival Comedies of Hans Sachs (1494–1576)*, Bristol German Publications 4 (Lewiston: Mellen, 1994). Robert W. Scribner gives an account of contemporary Wittenberg observance of the tradition in "Reformation, Carnival, and the World Turned Upside-Down," in *Städtische Gesellschaft und Reformation*, ed. Ingrid Bátori (Stuttgart: Klett-Cotta, 1980), pp. 234–64, especially 236–37.

[44] *daß man den Teufel nicht über die Tür male.* That is, one should not invite the devil's presence, as though by painting his image on a wall or above a door. See Oskar Brenner and Ernst Thiele in WA 51:657, 712, no. 356. Here, the rector and council should not invite the devil's presence by permitting sinful behavior at the Carnival plays.

[45] Nine guilders [*Gulden*] was a very high price to pay for any item of clothing. Some poorly paid pastors were given an annual salary of ten guilders. Luther was concerned about extravagance in dress around this time. See *Sermons on Matthew 18–24* (1537–40), AE 68:172, 337.

listened to preaching by way of Lot, yet they did not improve. So will it be with us as well.

We should be grateful to God, and everyone should serve God in his vocation. God may grant His grace for a rule of law to be established that the father of each family may govern his household, and preceptors their students; else I will make a cross above the pulpit.[46] But how have we come to the point where we are supposed to preach and no one wants to listen to us? When parents send their children here, they only want to go for a walk and use up their money. Then, when they are feasting and drinking to excess, someone pulls out a knife. But guard yourself, and bless yourself morning and evening,[47] and pray diligently, live in the fear of God. For it says in 1 Peter 5 [:8]: "The devil prowls around like a roaring lion, seeking whom he may devour."

Then, too, many are sent here to find out what we do here, and when something bad happens, they laugh at us in secret. Because I know this, I should pray, and know that the devil prowls around, and make sure that we do not end up like the people of Sodom. Guard yourself earnestly against the devil! Yet you would escape him only with difficulty. This complacency often results in someone getting into a situation which he did not foresee, as happened with Moses and St. Peter. However, listen to God's Word, and pray and walk in the fear of God; for the devil is a murderer and a liar [John 8:44].

For this reason, avoid coarse gatherings. Having a decent, good time and a drink are not forbidden as long as you do not become swine.

In Erfurt, I saw several people end miserably simply because they associated with bad company. The devil is not in Babylon but in my room—indeed, in my flesh and my heart. I know how close he is to me. He is deeper in my heart than even my prayer can be. He will be all the closer to you if you live complacently in sins. We have a very fine school, but we also have a villain or ten who are the mangy sheep.

I think that I must preach the First Commandment again [Exod. 20:3], for I hear some among us maintaining that a dead body should be laid on its face and the shoes put on the wrong way so that the perpetrator cannot escape.[48] This is written nowhere. It is simply putting God to the test and invoking and worshiping the devil. Then you will have a pact with the devil.

---

[46] The sign of the cross was a gesture of either blessing or of protection against evil. Here Luther seems to mean he would avoid preaching to the people.

[47] Luther gave a form for blessing oneself morning and evening in the *Small Catechism* (1529) Morning and Evening Prayer (Kolb-Wengert, pp. 363–64; *Concordia*, p. 344).

[48] This was a superstitous practice intended to prevent the spirit of the deceased from escaping from the grave (see WA 46:178 n. 4).

I do not want to take those sins on myself either. It is no help that we have God's Word; God will punish us all the more terribly.

Fifth Sermon on Holy Baptism, on Sexagesima Sunday February 24, 1538

Matthew 3:1–17

This text is long.[49] But up till now we have heard these three points: first, Baptism was instituted by God Himself; second, it is a washing with water, or baptizing, along with God's Word; third, the power and virtue of Baptism is that it cleanses people from sins and delivers them from death. Christians must learn this so that they may know how to hold Baptism in high esteem and view it with true earnest and Christian eyes, and know accordingly that the devil does not sleep but is continually raising his specter along with it in order that people may forget the benefit and use of holy Baptism, as truly happened in the papacy shortly after St. Augustine's time, when other customs came to be used more and more alongside Baptism, as it also says in Colossians 2 [:8]. Therefore, the apostles admonished us not to be led away from Christ, for He is our Head, and we are His members [cf. Eph. 1:22; 4:15]. This admonition was helpful to the righteous and God-fearing. But the others, whose ears were scratched, fell away, as stated in 2 Timothy 4 [:3–4]. Hence the whole world was filled with monasteries, for it impresses the world when someone goes around wearing a gray cowl, eating vegetables, and drinking water. This began shortly after the apostolic era, and they were amazing and terrible, great works. By contrast, Baptism had a lowly appearance and reputation, for it is a handful of water. Therefore, it was despised. But here it should be seen that good, godly bishops and Christians distinguish between what God instituted and what was instituted by men and proceeds according to human statutes and according to the world's statutes and not according to Christ, as stated in Colossians [2:8]. And though St. Francis or even an angel from heaven extol it, look to see whether it comes from their own choosing and the will of man, or whether it was commanded from heaven. Then you will find that all the orders of Saints Francis, Bernard, Augustine, and Benedict and others were only an

[49] Translated by Matthew Carver from Martin Luther, *Ungedruckte Predigten D. Martin Luthers aus den Jahren 1537–1540*, ed. Georg Buchwald (Leipzig: G. Strübigs Verlag, 1905), pp. 294–300. Cf. the stenographic notes for this sermon in WA 46:179–85 (Aland Pr 1699). The reading for the sermon was Matthew 3, the entire chapter (WA 46:179.1).

adopted way of life and chosen of people's own accord.[50] Later they added the three vows of chastity, poverty, and obedience. This is nothing other than what was pleasing to them, for which he had an opinion, and none other than the opinion of a man at that. But they say, "It is a good opinion all the same!" Hear St. Paul say about this, whenever someone undertakes something of his own choosing, and adds something of his own presumption, even if he should be an angel from heaven: "Let him be accursed" [Gal. 1:8]. But it may well happen that many of those who gladly lived in such a manner were saved. Yet for someone to make a sin out of not keeping this opinion, statute, and adopted manner of life—or to make it righteousness if someone follows and lives in accordance with it—that is wrong. I will certainly let you be a monk and wear a cowl if that is your desire, as long as you say that you will not become a holy man thereby but that it pleases you—for you cling to the Head, Christ, and to Baptism, which did not come from the will or thinking of man. I can also say, "I will remain a virgin, or be a widow and wear black, for it pleases me to do so," as long as you do not make a law that it is a sin if you abandon it, or say that you become righteous and good in God's sight if you do it. For it is an adopted way of life and your own choice. It should not be given the honor of washing away sin, nor should the devil be set above God and the pope above the apostles. For this reason we are to distinguish that which God directed and what is devised by man. St. John [1:13] says that the children of God are born not according to blood (like the Israelites) nor according to the will of the flesh (and if it is the will of the flesh or of the man, it is invalid, no matter how beautifully it gleams). St. Bernard had a desire to remain in his cowl. Yet do not turn it into a holy order. For those are all additions of the devil. Rather, cling only to Christ, that by Him you may be cleansed from sin. But if you add something to that, [it is wrong]: "I am a Beguine, so I am better than another woman."[51] This is seen in Saints Gregory, Anthony, and others.[52] Neither should one

[50] St. Francis of Assisi (ca. 1181–1226) founded the Franciscan order of mendicant preachers. Augustine's name was attached to several religious orders. Benedict of Nursia (ca. 480–ca. 547) established a religious community in Monte Cassino, Italy, in about 525. He later (ca. 540) wrote his *Rule*, a collection of straightforward organizing principles for a community of monks, which was eventually adopted by other monastic communities. Bernard of Clairvaux (1090–1153) was the most famous member of the Cistercian Order, which was a reform of Benedictine monasticism.

[51] Beguines were Christian laywomen who gathered into organized associations that flourished especially in the thirteenth and fourteenth centuries, often under the guidance of Dominican or Franciscan friars, for purposes of devotion and of charitable work, including some spiritual care, from which they were called "soul-women" in Germany and the Low Countries. See *ODCC*, 3rd ed., s.v. "Beguines, Beghards."

[52] I.e., Pope Gregory the Great (r. 590–604) and Anthony of Egypt (ca. 251–356), who is considered the founder of Christian monastic life.

take them as an example: "St. Ambrose lived without a wife; therefore, I will not have a wife either." Please, do not make a rule of it for me! Likewise, if you wear a black frock, wear it, and do not make a rule of it for me! For the pope did so also and confirmed his own choice and opinion. Hence all the monasteries sprang up and were built so that we could be participants in their good works and merits. This was not commanded by God, but they chose it themselves. Therefore, he says here: "Go, and may it please you! Only make no state of righteousness or sin out of it for me." I will listen instead to Christ and what He says, for He has a command from heaven that I should listen to Him [Matt. 3:17]. If we did that, we would have remained pure in Baptism and the Supper along with all the other things that Christ left behind for us, and would then remain in cities and not go off to isolated cloisters, or to Rome and Santiago, and would have remained married. But the devil labored long until Holy Scripture was thrown under the bench[53] and the Virgin Mary and other saints were appointed as our saviors and mediators instead of the Lord Christ.

Therefore, let us make sure that we remain in what He has commanded and instituted. For everything else is an adopted way of life, and if the pope wishes to interpret Holy Scripture, pastors should see to it that they take his false interpretation away from him. St. Peter says that no prophecy or prediction came from the choice, thinking, or will of man [2 Pet. 1:21]. In other words, I should examine a doctrine to see whether it is the choice or thinking and invention of man. If it is, then it is not a prophecy, for no prophecy came from the will of man. Yet the world is filled with such prophecies, but they are the prophecies which please men and which men have chosen, and though for appearance's sake they may refer to Holy Scripture, be alert and watch that you do not apply the Scripture to a false interpretation invented by men. But you can be assured whenever God has said and commanded something, such as when Christ says, "Go into the world and preach the Gospel to all creatures. Whoever believes and is baptized will be saved" [Mark 16:15–16]. Likewise, the Lord Christ was baptized and commanded that we should do as He did, in the name of the Father, Son, and Holy Spirit. There I know for certain that it is not my interpretation. It is the same way with the Sacrament of the Altar and with the Absolution or power of the Keys: if I desire to be comforted and am absolved of sins, I am sure that my will is interpreting nothing, but God says, "Whose sins you shall loose on earth, to him they are loosed in heaven also" [John 20:23; cf. Matt. 16:19; 18:18]. Here, then, I follow the ordinance of God and refrain from that which men may choose.

---

[53] One of Luther's favorite expressions for neglect of God's Word.

It seems like an excellent thing when we hear: "Such was the life of St. Gregory and St. Bernard—people who beyond all doubt were saved." Here someone says, "Were our fathers all fools?" But the apostle St. Paul says, "You must not look to any saint, for even if he is an angel from heaven, let him be accursed if he tries to bring his own choice" [cf. Gal. 1:8]. He is welcome to use it as long as he does not make a way to salvation out of it, much less compel others, but sticks to God's Word. For it is by this that God wishes to be with us. I am shrewd and know well what damage it does when God's Word is not handled purely. Great people fail in this regard and are led astray.

I will accordingly deal with the text, beginning with the last words. The final part of chapter 3 [of Matthew] deals with the Baptism of Christ. For in the first part, he shows what John the Baptist preached to the Jews. Now the Lord Christ is in His thirtieth year, or entering upon His thirtieth year, and has kept silent for thirty years, and is now to begin His kingdom and glory, or the office of high priest. Therefore, He leaves Capernaum, where He lived some twenty years. But before this, John was preaching in the wilderness that they should repent, for the kingdom of God was at hand [Matt. 3:2]. He was His forerunner, and therefore he had to wear distinct clothing and not eat bread or drink wine [Matt. 3:4], not because he was trying to obtain righteousness before God by such a strict way of life, but in order that the people would be exhorted by it and persuaded to listen to him and to believe his teaching. For his preaching was not to be done in secret, nor was John to remain unknown. Therefore, by such external masks the people were directed to John. Yet he does not insert his leather belt into his teaching. He has the townspeople and peasants stay in the cities and does not say that they are to eat honey and use his diet. He does not turn his life into a rule, but draws himself and all people to one name, Christ, and has no desire that they should follow his way of life, but rather his teaching, and says, "I did not come to preach about myself and that you may be your own masters. No, I did not come for that. I do not wish to be regarded that way. Rather, there is one who is stronger than I, and He is just outside the door. It is to Him that I direct you, and bid you to repent" [cf. Matt. 3:11–12]. You are to do these two things: repent and believe the Gospel. Therefore, his belt is of no concern to us. I have seen monks who were called Johannites, who tried to live according to John's external conduct, and dismissed the Lord Christ to whom he pointed. We are not to look to John nor imitate his life, but to pay attention to Him to whom he points with his finger. Thus John the Baptist first calls people to repent; second, to receive Christ, who brings forgiveness of sins, saying, "Repent!" [Matt. 3:2], that is, "Confess that you are stuck in sin, and even if you sacrifice and pray day and night, it is no use." Here the word "Repent" applies to all, no one is excluded; for whoever lives outside of Christ should know that he is in a sinful condition and cannot be saved unless he acknowledges that he is in a sinful condition. And John preached at the same time to the Pharisees and said to them that they were living in a sinful condition [cf. Matt. 3:7]. We are worse than they, for we bore the abomination of the papacy and nevertheless called it a state of perfection.[54] So if he could say this to the Pharisees and learned men in the temple, much more should it be said to the Carthusian also.[55] "If you are outside of Christ, then know that you are a sinner, condemned and lost," says John. Second, he says, "Make sure to receive Christ in faith."

This is the preaching of John the Baptist, and those who now heard about the preaching came from Jerusalem and were baptized. For when they believed the preaching of John, they confessed that they were sinners, just as we do today at children's Baptisms, when the children say, "I renounce the devil."[56] After that they are baptized and listen to Christ. It must be so. This is how John preached, and this is how we still teach and defend ourselves from all sects and in this way beat down sin and death. For outside of Christ there is no salvation or blessedness. Be it Carthusian or whatever you please, it is all human thinking, opinion, and personal choice. Now when John means that Christ is coming for Baptism, John's Baptism becomes a far different Baptism, and he says, "I baptize you with water, and I baptize for repentance" [Matt. 3:11]. His words provide a good understanding of Baptism. He says, "I baptize you with water, yet only such that all of you who wish to listen to and receive Christ receive Baptism." Thus he relates his Baptism to Christ, so that those who believed and were baptized by John's Baptism were saved, for John's Baptism points to Christ. All the patriarchs and prophets were also saved in this way, for they had the promise that they were to be circumcised, and then hoped in and waited for Christ. All believers have been saved in the same way, for their faith has stood on the Person on whom our faith still depends.

John's Baptism, then, is only a sign of repentance and gives the people the consolation that the true Savior would soon be coming. In this way the baptized were saved, for they had faith in the coming Christ. But once Christ has come, Baptism refers to the Christ who has come, and if someone now

[54] On monasticism as a "state of perfection," see Thomas Aquinas, *ST*, 2–2 qq. 184, 186 (Blackfriars 47:19–58, 97–144), citing earlier writers such as John Cassian (ca. 360–ca. 430/5).

[55] Founded by Bruno of Cologne (ca. 1030–1101) in 1084 in Grand Chartreuse, France, Carthusians are a famously strict order that requires silence, labor, and contemplative prayer. Luther often referred to them as exemplars of the most intensive form of ascetic life.

[56] See Luther, *Order of Baptism* (1523), AE 53:99; *Order of Baptism Newly Revised* (1526), AE 53:108–9.

wished to be baptized into the coming Christ, that baptism would not be right; for they believed in the coming Christ, and in the present one they were all saved. This is the manner and institution of our Lord God. This is why Matthew writes that John's Baptism ceases when Christ is there and wishes to fulfill the word and preaching of John. And John says:

"*I need to be baptized by You*" [Matt. 3:14]. This is great humility. He knows the person of whom he had preached until now, and that He would become King and High Priest and assume the office of the Messiah, as the angel names Him: "To you is born Christ the Lord" [Luke 2:11]. "Christ," that is, "Anointed One," King, and High Priest, for He is both a preacher and a king, anointed not with chrism[57] but with the Holy Spirit. Here the office begins and embraces in the name "Christ" those who belong to God. Before He was called only "Jesus" [Matt. 1:21], but He has Himself baptized and comes out and preaches and sacrifices Himself on the cross and becomes our High Priest who reigns over us forever, and no one else but He can bear the name "Christ." All other kings and priests were anointed, but this one has an anointing different from that of David and Aaron or the other kings and high priests. For the Holy Spirit is upon Him, as we see here in the Baptism [Matt. 3:16]. Therefore, He becomes a true High Priest and King, and enters publicly into His office, and says to John: "Please, be at peace! It is commanded that I must be baptized, and it is right that you do it, that I may be baptized by you, for I will do what the Father has commanded Me" [cf. Matt. 3:15]. Yet Christ is not baptized because He needed it or to obtain righteousness and salvation by it. Why, then, did He do it? In truth, not only as an example for us, but to make us a strong, holy, and powerful bath by touching the Jordan with His body and in this way blessing our Baptism. Now we know that a washing was there prepared for us, such that whoever is baptized has forgiveness of sins and the washing away of sins and redemption from death. For this reason, Baptism was given to the whole world, that whoever wishes to be saved might wash in the same bath in which Christ also stood. And there I get the innocence which He brought into the bath, and the world also obtains His innocence, life, and honor, and it is not a human choice. Is this not a great glory that he who is baptized receives these things? John's Baptism does not do it, but Christ's Baptism. John could not make a Baptism like that, but he points to Him who made it, and it is nevertheless the same Baptism in which the Holy Spirit and the gifts of the Holy Spirit are apportioned and the body is cleansed of its sins and ushered into eternal life.

This is why the Baptism is portrayed in such a way that, as the Lord Christ is coming up from the water, heaven opens [Matt. 3:16]. Behold, how

[57] See above, p. 22 n. 17.

God adorns Baptism! He flaunts no jewels or gold, and yet who can describe the splendor here? Here is the entire Holy Trinity: the Son in the water, the Father in the word, and the Holy Spirit in the form of a dove. The true, divine Majesty is present in three forms; the Son is in the human nature. Whoever does not care to look at this, let him look to St. Francis in a cowl! But what is all the personal choosing of the monks compared to this majesty and glory of God? The former is all an adopted way of life. No one is washed clean of his sins by wearing a cowl, for in the monastic "baptism," God the Father, Son, and Holy Spirit is not present. But here the kingdom and priesthood are confirmed, for here is the Son of God, as the Father says:

"*This is My beloved Son*" [Matt. 3:17]. Mark these words well. If you want to know where God's will and heart are, do not look to St. Francis's cowl or to the holiness of the Turks or to the religion of the Papists, but "This is My beloved Son," who is being baptized by John. Now then, if He is the Son, He is Lord of all lords and King. He is true man, born of the Virgin Mary, and yet also true God. Both of these are seen here. "This is My beloved Son in whom I am well pleased." For whatever else is outside the Son is indignation, wrath, and disfavor. Therefore, John, with this word, draws all to the one Christ, so that if we wish to have God's grace, will, and good-pleasure, we are to pay attention to the Son, for He is our High Priest and King.

Such, then, is Christ's Baptism, that John does not point to Him who is to come but to Him who has come, and the Holy Spirit anoints Him with Himself, and He is called by the Father and the Holy Spirit to enter into His office, saying, "Here we have the highest King and Priest, and whoever is able to believe in Him, let him believe and seek no other way to come to Me!" This is why Paul was angry and says, "Let him be accursed" [Gal. 1:8]—even if it should be an angel from heaven—who brings another teaching than the one which God the heavenly Father teaches here. St. Peter says the same [2 Pet. 1:17–21]: This is the Son of God. This is certain, and you do well to believe this word. For false prophets will come, preaching according to human choosing, and will cause the world to be filled with factions. Therefore, remain in the sure word which we ourselves heard come down from heaven here. For in the Son is all great grace and good-pleasure, and it is resolved that whoever remains in Him surely has eternal life and a gracious God. For when people depend on human traditions and choices, especially with the condition that God's grace and good-pleasure will be obtained thereby, it is all over. But see grace and good-pleasure only in Christ, then you have forgiveness of sins. But the Turks and Carthusians do great works and act as if they were living angels, yet it is all in vain. God's grace will not be found there. It is not sought in Rome or Santiago. But God has sufficiently affirmed it, and the place, time, and person, saying, "This is My beloved Son." This was not done in secret, but has even been proclaimed to the whole world. But the world despises it and follows after other ways. Therefore, whoever wishes to be saved, let him cling to Baptism, in which we are baptized in the name of the Father, Son, and Holy Spirit. There are three persons, the true God, who baptizes us. Man adds nothing to it. Aside from that, take up whatever external matters you wish, and let the choosing proceed! Buy a house, and if you do not want to sow barley in the field, use wheat! But in the matters of God, to escape sin and become righteous, nothing that you choose helps. Rather, cling to the Son, listen to Him, and make sure nothing tears you away from Him, be it saints, angels, or whoever, but plug your ears! The Father pointed us only to the Son. We should keep this word with great diligence and act according to it, and believe it, and shun and flee from all else, no matter how glorious and excellent it may seem.

Sixth Sermon on Holy Baptism, on *Estomihi* Sunday March 3, 1538

I[58] have seen what kind of damage results from not keeping the doctrine of the sacraments correctly, so let us at this time continue to preach on Baptism. The text says, "When Jesus was baptized and came up from the Jordan, the heavens opened, and the Holy Spirit appeared in the form of a dove, and a voice came from the clouds, saying, 'This is My beloved Son, in whom I am well pleased'" [Matt. 3:16–17]. This verse should be remembered well, for no washing of the Jews and Turks nor consecrated water of the pope can compare to Baptism, for none of them was instituted by God. The Turk has a great deal of washings, and the pope, too, has his consecrated water, which Pope Alexander V instituted,[59] but let him keep washing with his water and leave me in peace! Baptism, however, is a divine washing and consists of two things: the Word of God and the water. And the Word makes Baptism so glorious that whoever is baptized in it is washed and cleansed with the blood of Christ. For this reason Baptism is to be reckoned so glorious as is

[58] Translated by Matthew Carver from Martin Luther, *Dr. Martin Luther's Sämmtliche Werke*, 2nd series, vol. 20, part 1, ed. Ernst Ludwig Enders (Frankfurt am Main: Heyder & Zimmer, 1880), pp. 66–74. Cf. the stenographic notes for this sermon in WA 46:194–201 (Aland Pr 1701).

[59] At Luther's time, the institution of holy water as a sacramental was often traced to Ps.-Alexander I (r. 105–115), in *Decretum Gratiani* 3.3.20, in Aemilius Friedberg, ed., *Corpus Iuris Canonici*, editio Lipsiensis secunda, 2 vols. (Graz: Akademische Druck- u. Verlagsanstalt, 1959), vol. 1, col. 1358. Luther or his editors misread *Alexander Papa V. a Petro* ("Alexander, the fifth pope after Peter") as meaning "Pope Alexander V."

the blood of Christ. Furthermore, the Word of Christ endues Baptism with the power of Christ's suffering. Consecrated water does not have this Word. Thus Baptism confers and brings the washing away of sin or the forgiveness of sin; likewise, the drowning of death and the putting on of the garment which is called eternal life, for the sake of Him who instituted Baptism and is the mighty Lord; and does not institute for us or distribute to us anything small or insignificant. And although it seems insignificant, it should not mislead us. For this reason we should examine Baptism with spiritual eyes.

Finally, we will also add to this and expound from the text: "This is My beloved Son, in whom I have good-pleasure" [Matt. 3:17]. St. Jerome, one of the four doctors of the Church, says that when a man falls into sin after Baptism, he should turn to penance, which he likens to a plank left over from a shipwreck, which a man takes hold of and on it swims ashore.[60] Thus when I am baptized, I am in a ship, and if I sin, the ship is wrecked. Here you might ask, how will I be saved? To this he replies, "You must take hold of the plank and swim out of it."

This was repeated again and again, and led the church to the false understanding that sins rendered Baptism wholly invalid and it was necessary for us to resort to penance. Now if I understood the word "penance"[61] as the pope uses it, it is far worse. Then my salvation would have to depend on my good works. In this way, Baptism was polluted and of no benefit unless sufficient penance had been done. And thus, after sinning, we were directed to our own work, meaning that Baptism is a washing which lasts and counts only until someone sins and falls. For this reason the mindless people kept teaching that Baptism washed away only original sin, and that the blood of Christ serves for the expiation of original sin, but if we sin after that, we must do penance. Then it necessarily followed that saints were sought and chosen as patrons, helpers in need, and intercessors, for Baptism and the blood of Christ had been utterly taken away, and Christ had been made into nothing more than a stern judge. And then the people went far astray, for one went off into the wilderness and became a hermit, another ate no meat and drank no wine, or else became a Carthusian, Franciscan, or Dominican.[62] This was all described as "doing penance," for God was angry and the sufferings and death of the Lord Christ were of no use. Therefore, they crept around in foolscaps[63] and resorted to the superfluous good works of monks and priests. This is why so many churches and altars were built;

---

[60] See above, "To the Christian Reader," p. ix.

[61] *Buße*, or "repentance."

[62] See above, p. 87 n. 50, p. 90 n. 55. The Dominicans, or Order of Preachers, was founded by Dominic de Guzmán (ca. 1170–1221).

[63] Derisively, for monastic cowls and vestments.

this is all still before our eyes. In time, purgatory was invented—a huge, mighty, desolate thing! Neither could it be otherwise, since Baptism and the Lord Christ had been lost. Then came having contrition[64] for sin; likewise, confessing every sin and making satisfaction for sin. This is all directing people to themselves.

This is why it is necessary to preach carefully that Baptism does not cease, for Baptism is an eternal covenant with Christ that He will be our Savior, Mediator, Bishop, and Archshepherd [1 Pet. 5:4] of our soul. The covenant does not cease, because the Lord Christ is seated at the right hand of His Father and lives. In this passage, moreover, it is written that He is Lord of all lords, for the heavenly Father has given Him the kingdom of heaven, and whoever wishes to have a gracious God and Father in heaven must listen to this Son [cf. Matt. 17:5]. For where Christ is not Mediator, God is a consuming fire. For this reason He has placed before our eyes a pleasant image, namely, a *human nature* like ourselves, and we are glad to see it, especially in our time of need. Neither has God willed to put before us any other figure or image than our own nature, that it might be our *umbraculum*, our "shelter and shade" [cf. Isa. 4:6], under which we might be safe from the wrath of God. This covenant does not cease. When I am baptized, I am under the heaven or shelter of grace, and the wrath of God cannot touch me; for He has relinquished the rule and handed it over to His Son, and through Baptism I enter into His kingdom.

Accordingly, the kingdom of Christ, which He established by His humanity, continues in this way until the Last Day, and Baptism continues in the same form also, and we live under His shadow so that the wrath of God can do us no harm. Therefore, think: "O Lord Jesus Christ! The devil and sin have seized me from Your kingdom, but You are still seated in the covenant and grace which You showed me." Therefore, while I may fall out of it, He remains seated, and even though I stumble and sin, the covenant of Baptism is not therefore false.

When repentance[65] is preached in this way, it is correct: namely, that a sinner turn back to the Mercy Seat, Christ, and not think: "Alas, Christ is no longer my Reconciler, Mediator, or Mercy Seat" or "His suffering and death are in vain!" Otherwise they would be following the monks, who ended up with their own good works. That is then the repentance of Judas! Rather, turn back to the kingdom of grace which God established through Christ and through Him brought to completion. By Baptism you have become a citizen of this kingdom, so remain in it. But if you fall out of it, see that you go back into it. When a prince makes a contract or covenant with freeholders

[64] *Reu*, or "remorse."

[65] *Buße*

to be their lord and they his subjects, and a subject breaks some part of the covenant, he abandons it, but the covenant does not therefore cease. A prince does not nullify a covenant because someone breaks and transgresses it. Such is not the way of the world. The covenant becomes stronger, because the lord, desiring his covenant to be kept, punishes those who refuse to obey. But if someone is a good man, he says, "I have done wrong by stepping outside of the covenant; therefore, I will fall at the feet of my lord and beg for grace and pardon." This man returns to the covenant from which he fell. Thus this covenant is not breached because of his abandonment, but remains firm as before.

Something similar happens also when I fall from Christ and act against Baptism. In such a case, I should kneel down and say, "I sin; yet, dear Lord Christ, be my Mediator and High Priest!" Then you enter again the kingdom of grace and mercy where Christ is king; then He eagerly welcomes you back. As in fact the Lord Christ says to the Christian Church: "Whosesoever sins you will release on earth, to them will they be released in heaven" [John 20:23; cf. Matt. 16:19; 18:18]. But if someone wished to say, "I have sinned against the Lord Christ. I will not find any grace; therefore, I will seek another lord," and fought against His covenant and the power of his Lord, as do all apostates[66] of the Church, that is too far. Therefore, if you fall out of Christ's kingdom and refuse to enter the covenant again, and become mad and foolish and fight and rave against Christ, that is wrong. A Carthusian similarly thinks when he has sinned: "I do not want to be with Christ anymore; I will start earning grace myself!" This is also how the Turks and all the monks think, saying, "I have sinned, but let God regard my strict life and be my gracious God on that account!" Then they take the Lord Christ for a stern judge. But what does God the heavenly Father say to that? He says, "Cursed are you and all your works! I sent you My Son as your High Priest and Mediator that He might be your King and Savior, but you tried to make Him your Judge and propitiate Me with your stinking, lousy works!" Then God must in turn become a consuming fire, for it says in our text: "This is My beloved Son!" Therefore, if we are not under Christ, we are under judgment, and even if all the teachers of works were there, it would still mean nothing. For the villain brings me from Christ and the covenant not only to good works but also to rebellion against Christ. But only Christ is our Savior. He redeemed us from sin. I am to enter into the covenant and remain in it; but if I fall out of it, I am to go back to it and regard Christ as the Bishop of our souls [1 Pet. 2:25]. For this reason, anything that people devise contrary to this doctrine is folly, and not only do they lose Christ, but they even fight against Him. So God says, "This is My beloved Son. Listen to

[66] *Mammelucken und Apostatae*

Him!" [cf. Matt. 17:5]. Whoever tries to get to heaven without this Son finds only God's wrath. Thus in the papacy I go along in such a way that Christ's suffering and death are absent and even Baptism is nothing. Therefore, one man became a Franciscan and another entered some other order. This is nothing but a pagan and Turkish faith.

Thus, through their ignorance, the fathers turned Christians into utter pagans. For they did not know of the essence, nature, power, and operation of Baptism. And what we should know is this: when I fall out of Baptism, I take myself out; but then I cannot undertake some new work, but must go back under my dear Lord Christ. And if the kite has chased me away from my mother hen, I crawl back under her wings [cf. Matt. 23:37]. But if I take up another order, whatever it may be called, I may be sure that, since God did not establish it, it is the devil, and I am not merely disobeying Christ but even persecuting Him. This is the origin of the terrible and detestable ignorance about Baptism, in which it was not rightly understood. Yet we should know that Baptism is an eternal covenant by which we are enrolled in the citizenry under Christ the King, who does not break apart but is everlasting.

Therefore, learn that Baptism is nothing temporary, as the world sees it with its carnal eyes, imagining that Baptism avails only once. But know that by Baptism you enter into an eternal covenant, and even if you sin, you have Baptism behind you. Go back into it. Christ does not fall from His throne even though you sin. Be afraid, then, because you have fallen from Christ, but enter into the covenant again, and do not say, "I will take up a new order in which I will do many good works so that God will forgive my sins." No! You must return to the covenant of Baptism and say, "I fell out of it, but I will take hold again of the ship that does not break apart." For the price is the kingdom of Christ, which is not lost on account of your fall.

In this way we might guard ourselves against the sects, which do not understand Christ's kingdom or Baptism but think that penance is a plank from the broken ship. The covenant cannot be lost, nor can Christ's kingdom be broken asunder. You are baptized and belong to this kingdom, so even if you fall out of it, you are free to enter it again and begin to believe in Christ once more. For we must persevere in believing that Christ has made satisfaction for our sins. They did not teach this, but claimed that if I sin after Baptism, I have lost Christ and my chance at His kingdom. Now it is certainly true that I have truly lost Christ; but Christ is present, and I can obtain and procure His kingdom and covenant again. Thus the apostles preached that Christ is the Mediator before the Father. This He is not only once, when someone receives Baptism, but continually. For thus says St. John in his Epistle: "If anyone sins"—what do we do? Do we run to the desert? No—"we have an Advocate with God, who is faithful," etc. [1 John 2:1].

Repentance, then, is preached rightly when people are brought to Christ the High Priest, and I am not directed to beginning some peculiar and new thing with my own works. I have entered Christ's kingdom where I possess a gracious High Priest [Heb. 4:14], but those who do not believe in Him become sectarian spirits. To us, however, He will say, "You have believed in Me; therefore, you shall be saved." But He will judge the others who do not believe in Him.

This saying of Jerome's has done visible damage, so that we cannot trust the fathers very much. It would be fitting for this passage of Jerome to be buried for a thousand years; then the Church or the kingdom of Christ will not be shattered, nor the covenant of Baptism be blotted out.

At the same time that they began to administer Baptism to infants, it was argued that children should not be baptized but should wait until they grow up. And St. Augustine's mother was unwilling to have her son baptized until he reached the age of reason and was mature, if he were good; then she would have him baptized. But what happened? Augustine grew worse as time went on, and became a crude, undisciplined heathen, and finally despised Baptism, the apostles, and the prophets and became a Manichaean.[67] Then it was the parents' counsel and opinion that Augustine should not be baptized without first understanding it. In that time, there was the delusion that Baptism was something temporary, and Baptism should not be given before children reached the age of reason. And St. Augustine writes that he had a good friend, with whom he used to play, who became sick. And when Augustine mocked him for having been baptized (just as he used to laugh at others), his friend responded to the contrary, saying, "Leave me alone. Do not say such things!" Then St. Augustine marveled and was troubled, for he saw that his playmate had turned to Christ in his heart.

Others were reluctant to give Baptism except when people were lying on their deathbed. And Emperor Constantine put off his own Baptism until he was ready to die. They were all of the opinion which St. Jerome also held. The world was eventually swallowed up by this idea. God grant that we may keep well this text, in which God the Father says to the one being baptized: "All My love, good-pleasure, and mercy is in the Son. And he who is found outside the Son is in disfavor, and he who is not in the Son is condemned and lost." For the Father placed all things in Him as the Light, Truth, and Life of men [cf. John 8:12; 14:6]. He was to be King over heaven and earth, and yet at the same time our gracious God. And the Father says, "If you wish to

[67] This heretical system (following the teachings of Mani [ca. 216–276]) rejected the material world as evil, considered Jesus to be a divine emissary sent to liberate the souls of men from material entrapment, and believed that Jesus' humanity was only apparent. Augustine, a former Manichaean, became the principal orthodox opponent of this teaching.

rejoice in My good-pleasure, you have it there." Therefore, even if I fall out of the covenant which Christ made with me, He is not broken apart. Only see that you turn back to Christ, and do not view Him as a hostile judge, for He will continue to be the King of grace until the end of the world, not momentarily or for the blink of an eye. Rather, by the washing of Baptism You enter into an eternal covenant. So if you fall out of it, the washing does not fall out after you. Here I am to remember that I return through contrition, sorrow, and faith, but not through my works.

This is what we wished to say about the third point, and I add to this that it is an eternal covenant. If I fall out of it, I enter again in faith, believing that Christ died for me. If you try to take up your own work of satisfaction as the monks do, you will perish; no saint was ever addressed with the words "You are My beloved Son," etc. Moreover, you would then be fighting against Christ and trying to storm His kingdom. Now then, God established the covenant. If we turn away from it, we are condemned, but the covenant will remain forever.

CHAPTER FOUR

SERMONS ON HOLY BAPTISM (1539)

First Sermon on Holy Baptism, on the Feast of Epiphany January 6, 1539

In recent days[1] we have said in our preaching that we should know what we may or may not believe, in order that we may abide by the articles of our Christian faith[2] which we pray daily with our children when we say, "I believe in Jesus Christ, who was conceived by the Holy Spirit, born of the Virgin Mary."[3] For the devil is constantly looking for ways to suppress this article.

Now, it is our custom every year to preach about Baptism on this day. For three different subjects are considered and treated on this day: first, that the three Wise Men from the East came bearing gifts for the infant Christ; and, second, concerning Christ's Baptism; and, third, the miracle of His turning water into wine at the wedding in Cana of Galilee. For it is thought that all three events took place on the same day.

Of utmost necessity, however, is that the doctrine of Baptism be preserved in the Church. For it was severely obscured under the papacy, and still the devil does not rest but is eager to deprive children of Baptism. Indeed, he would like to banish it from the world completely. He produces nothing but lying and murder. For this reason everyone should know well what Baptism

[1] Translated by Matthew Carver from Martin Luther, *Ungedruckte Predigten D. Martin Luthers aus den Jahren 1537–1540*, ed. Georg Buchwald (Leipzig: G. Strübigs Verlag, 1905), pp. 500–505. Cf. the stenographic notes for this sermon in WA 47:640–46 (Aland Pr 1861).

The "recent days" to which Luther refers are December 29, 1538, and January 1 and 5, 1539, when he delivered three sermons on John 1:1–14 (WA 46:531–37; 47:628–34, 634–40; Aland Pr 1749, 1859, 1860).

[2] *Gaubens*, or "creed."

[3] The Second Article of the Apostles' Creed (Kolb-Wengert, p. 21; *Concordia*, p. 16).

is and where it comes from. So let us look at Matthew 3 [:13–17], where John the Baptist is preaching and the Lord Christ comes to him and is baptized by him. Grant that I could speak the very same words about Baptism every year which I used another year!

Now, in Baptism there are three things to consider, even as within Baptism itself there is a Trinity. First, it is not an invention of man as is consecrated water or the ablution of the Turks, or as was the Jewish purification which required a great deal of washing each day. Rather, a strong distinction must be made here, and we must say, "No matter whether you call it consecrated water, spiritual washing, or what you please, it is of no concern to me. I want to know whether it comes from man's own thinking or from God's command." For it is the cornerstone of our Christian doctrine that we tolerate nothing that man's reason invents, nor do we regard anything touching matters of our salvation unless it is God's Word and command. This is our foundation on which we stand against the pope and say, "Opinion does not matter! It does no good for you to say, 'I have good judgment,'" just as Saints Benedict and Francis instituted and established it from their own judgment and opinion.[4] A Christian should not think of basing his faith on his own judgment and opinion, nor on the revelation even of angels or saints [cf. Gal. 1:8], but on the sure Word of God, which comes from God. For so we pray in the Creed: "I believe in the Holy Spirit, the holy Christian Church."[5] Yet they call us "deserters of the Church" [*desertores ecclesiae*], whereas we, too, actually say that she is the holy Church, as the text of the Creed runs. But we say that the Church cannot be sanctified except by the Holy Spirit, since it does not come from one's own imagination or good intention but is a heavenly sanctification. For this reason the Holy Spirit is with her and dwells there. For there is Baptism, which is holy. She has the Word of God, which is holy, not a human invention; by it she is sanctified. She has the holy Supper, the Keys for opening and shutting; the Keys are holy too. Then the Holy Spirit is with the Church in a visible manner. Indeed, I can say further: you have the Ten Commandments, which are holy, and if you keep them, you will live and are holy also; you are being sanctified by them. The Lord's Prayer is holy. The estate of marriage is likewise created by God and therefore holy. In the same way, the estate of manservants and maidservants is all included in the Word of God; whoever occupies it is holy. Beyond these are the inventions of men which do not have the command of God, such as consecrated water, over which the Papists speak the Word of God, though doing so does not sanctify it.—"But they speak God's Word over it!"—Surely there is a great distinction, for they misuse the Word of God. God did not

[4] See above, p. 87 n. 50.

[5] The Third Article of the Apostles' Creed (Kolb-Wengert, p. 22; *Concordia*, p. 16).

command consecrated water. In the same way, the pope also sanctifies chasubles, hats, patens, altars, candles, cloths, wax, and the cowls of nuns and monks, and has made a great deal of sanctity in the church—let the devil thank him for it! Then he cries afterward that they are the holy Church and we have abandoned the Christian Church, but this we deny. For we seek the true Church and we have it, and we have the Word of God in its purity, Baptism in its purity, and the Supper in its purity, and we have the power to choose priests and ministers and to do all that pertains to the Church. It is not a sanctification that is done by men. Otherwise the Turks, Tatars,[6] and, indeed, sorcerers and witches would also be holy, for they sanctify themselves. We would not go so far as to preach here that the temple does not sanctify us but that we sanctify the temple. I do not sanctify Christ, Baptism, or Holy Scripture, but am sanctified by them. A child is not sanctified by his baptismal gown, but by Baptism. Similarly, we have the Church as a baptismal gown, in which the infant is wound as in swaddling cloths. Again, we retain the altar, corporal,[7] chalice,[8] pulpit, organ, missals,[9] and chants, but everything as an adornment and baptismal gown. Yet the chalice is not holy such that it would sanctify us. Therefore, we desire the holiness of the divine Word. For the Church becomes holy—namely, by the Holy Spirit—as we say, "I believe in the Holy Spirit." How does one come to the Holy Spirit? Should I not go to a monastery and become a Carthusian,[10] or go to Santiago as a pilgrim?[11] Where is that written? He does not come when you wish, but when He does come, receive Him. But how does He come? Baptism is holy. Who makes it holy? The Holy Spirit and the blood of Christ. For Baptism did not spring from my own heart, but was established from heaven, and the Holy Spirit sanctified this Baptism. Thus I find the Holy Spirit in Baptism. Again, I find Him in the holy Supper. For you receive not mere bread and wine but the flesh and blood of Christ. I do not seek the Holy Spirit, but He seeks me. The Supper is a holy thing,[12] and is holy, and by it the Holy Spirit makes people holy. In the same way, the Keys also are holy, when with the laying on of hands someone is made holy, not by human power but by the

---

[6] The Tatars were a Central Asian people, associated in the medieval European mind with the thirteenth-century Mongol conquests.

[7] An altar cloth for use in the Service of the Altar.

[8] The cup with which the blood of the Lord Jesus is distributed.

[9] *Meßbücher*, "Mass books." These were the service books with the pastor's words and music for the divine service.

[10] See above, p. 90 n. 55.

[11] See above, p. 64 n. 8.

[12] *Heiligtum*, a word which is also used for "holy relic," the mortal remains of saints, but can have a more general meaning as "holy thing" or "holy possession."

power of the Holy Spirit who instituted the Keys. Again, the preaching of the Gospel is not a human invention, for the Word of God was there before we were born. Thus wherever the Gospel is preached, the Holy Spirit comes and the Word sanctifies the Church. Again, if you do the Ten Commandments and attend to your vocation, God has ordered the estates and will be in them, and there also is the Holy Spirit.

Thus the Holy Spirit does not come to us by our own designs but has sufficiently appointed means by which He comes. For you have the Word, Baptism, the Supper, the Keys, the Ten Commandments; these are things of the Holy Spirit and not the worthless inventions of men. And whatever is outside of these articles the Holy Spirit has not established, and we use them only as it were swaddling cloths or a baptismal gown, which sanctify no one. Therefore, learn to defend yourselves against the cry of the pope, who says that he is the Church, and reply: "Very well, sir, you may be the church, but not the Christian or holy Church. And you are only holy by your own personal holiness, not the holiness of the Holy Spirit. Once that is established, we will gladly join you in the use of external things, as long as you do not turn them into commandments for us."—"Well, then," says the pope. "Believe in one church that is holy!" To this say, "Holy by your own holiness; but it is not enough for a church simply to be holy. It must also not be the Papist church, but that which knows Christ, has the Word of God, and accordingly suffers persecution and clings to His Word and Sacrament." Thus if I take up the cowl[13] and say, "I am a Christian and am holy," it is a denial and despising of Baptism and the blood of Christ, and by it Christ and all His benefits are trampled underfoot. I was brought up in the error of thinking that my Baptism was useless to me. This cancer was so deeply embedded in people's hearts they could not get rid of the idea, but thought that if anyone sinned after Baptism, it was useless to him. This preaching spread throughout the papacy, in which they still teach that one should undertake a "new Baptism" and enter a monastery. Bah! How could this rubbish ever be set higher than the Word of God and blood of Christ and institution of Baptism? Even if I have sinned and fallen, Baptism is not such a fleeting thing that it would no longer be any good. St. Jerome created a great stumbling block here by saying that penance is the plank that we take hold of in shipwreck and swim ashore, and are thereby saved.[14] This blasphemy spread in the papacy. Baptism was given to children, but for the mature and aged they said that Baptism was useless, and we should stake our lives on purifying ourselves by our works and by our washing—which

[13] I.e., become a monk.

[14] See above, "To the Christian Reader," p. ix.

would be to tear Christ completely out of our heart.[15] In the same way, pilgrimages and orders are sanctification, but human sanctification. God did not command and direct, but forbade us to trust in our works, and directed us to trust in the blood of Christ, by which we are redeemed. Going on pilgrimages was a tremendous lie. It is something invented, a good intention that God was supposed to regard and on that basis be gracious to someone. Holy Scripture presented the Virgin Mary to me not that I might be purified by her, but as she who brought our dear Savior into the world, that He might sanctify us. Therefore, she is worthy of all honor as the mother of God, but it is not for her to sanctify me, but for Him who is described thus in John 1:14: "The Word became flesh, full of grace and truth." The works of the Virgin Mary were bearing the Son and raising the Son. Those are different works from the works of the Lord Christ. Yet the Virgin Mary had greater honor in the papacy than her dear Son, the Lord Christ. I likewise had my heart set on her and attached to her. Therefore, make this distinction: the Church is holy and Christian. How? By the Holy Spirit. Well, then, will someone not also be holy if he goes to Santiago dressed in armor? That is a sanctification not by the Holy Spirit but by men, which is a holiness of dung. But I believe that I am sanctified as is the Christian Church. How is this done? Thus, when you say, "I believe in the Holy Spirit."—"Very well, how do I obtain Him?"—Do you not see Baptism and the Sacrament of the Supper? And do you not know how to pray the Lord's Prayer or how the Ten Commandments are to be kept? It is through these that you are sanctified. But if you glory in another sanctification, it is a work of dung, since it does not come from the Holy Spirit but is the holiness of man. It disguises itself as an angel of light [cf. 2 Cor. 11:14] and wears simple clothing, even as a Carthusian does. But you say, "I would be glad to wear a chasuble if only my own holiness may remain unscathed and these things do not conflict with true holiness." But the pope says, "If you will not believe that I am the head of the Church, you cannot be saved."[16] Where does this article of the Creed come from? What passage or verse of Scripture? It is from his own impudence and out of his own mind. For he says, "Because I am the head, you must and shall believe, on pain of your salvation, that whatever I decree is holy. I decree consecrated water and purgatory." But toss it out with the slop for the pigs to eat! If consecrated water were treated as something to refresh a man when he is weak, it would be fine. But as something to wash away sin? That is to set it above the blood of Christ, and the Lord Christ is diminished thereby. The Christian Church is she which believes in God and not in the pope, the holy

[15] Read with the punctuation of WA 47:643.20–22 instead of Buchwald, *Ungedruckte Predigten*, p. 503.

[16] See above, p. 81 n. 36.

Virgin, or a pastor or preacher. Otherwise it would be Peter's church, the pope's church, and so on. But that is not her real name. I do not believe in "one church of the holy Virgin," but in one Christian Church, and she is holy. How? Of herself? No, but by the blood of the Lord Christ. Then she asks for the forgiveness of sins.[17] Oh? How, then, is she holy? That is why I must look for the Holy Spirit, who is with her and governs her. He is not in a monastery or in St. Peter's in Rome, but in Baptism, in the Word that is preached, in the Keys and in a brother's mouth,[18] and also in the Ten Commandments, in the estate or vocation of a father, son, or daughter. [The Holy Spirit says,] "You will not find Me, but I will find you." The other trifles we can keep also, such as churches and altars, but we keep them as a baptismal gown.

Learn, therefore, as the first point, that Baptism was instituted by Christ, unlike consecrated water, the Jewish ablution, or the purification of the Turks or Tatars, which all come from the opinion and choice of man. Consecrated water is exactly the same as the water with which I wash my hands and body. "But they speak the Word of God over it!" Bah! Begone with the personal opinion that it purifies people! The devil is there. It is condemned because it is claimed to be a washing that purifies. But by the fact that [Baptism] is called the Baptism of the Holy Spirit and of Christ it is distinguished from all others. Christ is present in it, baptizing, and it is His Baptism. Therefore, it sanctifies, for the Holy Spirit wills to be present in it and has bound Himself to it, and Christ says to His disciples: "Go into all the world" [Matt. 28:19]. And the apostles used Baptism with these very words. Yet since God's command is there—"Go, baptizing"—the apostles do not create holy water, nor direct wood and stone to be baptized, but simply say, "We have a command that we are to baptize." Christ instituted Baptism, but the pope would gladly mislead us to his own holiness even as he has thereby misled the whole world.

Thus we have the use and proper understanding of the words of Baptism, the Ten Commandments, and the articles of our Christian Creed; likewise, the ordination of priests and everything else pertaining to the Christian Church. The only thing that we are missing now is the fasts, in order that we may live moderate and sober lives. I would gladly see authorities enact such a thing.[19] I also preach that we should live moderately, but I have no wish to make a ceremony out of it as with the pope's fasts, purgatory, and private Masses. Let us give no thought to them, for we are not made holy by them, nor are they holy, but only call themselves the holy Church.

---

[17] E.g., in the Fourth Petition of the Lord's Prayer (Kolb-Wengert, p. 357; *Concordia*, p. 335).

[18] Cf. *Smalcald Articles* (1537) III IV (Kolb-Wengert, p. 319; *Concordia*, p. 278).

[19] See above, Luther's "Admonition," pp. 82–86.

Thus we should know, first of all, that it is God's institution and God's commandment; second, that God's Word and water are present; third, the use. And you should say, "Those in the papacy may use St. John's Gospel[20] and pray many Our Fathers[21] and light wax candles.[22] But since it was not commanded by God, I will ignore it." If God had not commanded Baptism, it would be no different from consecrated water. Thus it is instituted by heaven, not invented by men.

Second Sermon on Holy Baptism, on the Second Sunday after Epiphany January 19, 1539

A[23] Christian should know the doctrine which we confess, upon which we are called and baptized, and upon which we are to die. Therefore, we should know what Baptism is and why or for what purpose a Christian is baptized. First of all, you have heard that there are three things to discuss in Baptism. The first is that we teach that Baptism would be nothing and just the same as consecrated water and a Turkish ablution if it did not have God's command. For then water would be mere water, and nothing would come of it. In the papacy, consecrated water was esteemed almost as equal to holy Baptism. As for yourself, say, "Does it also have God's command?" Where such cannot be demonstrated, there is the distinction between Baptism and all other washings and bathings. For it must have as its cornerstone the fact that it is commanded or instituted by God, or it is nothing at all. A bath makes us cleaner than Baptism can, but since it was not commanded by God, it is nothing. You should grasp this point firmly. However, if it is viewed as a human work, like consecrated water and bathroom water, it is nothing. But be sure yourself that it came from heaven, or it is nothing. For example, whores and rakes[24] live together, raise children, and collect property. This behavior and life is so

[20] John 1:1–14 was used at times as an amulet. See AE 46:135 n. 99.

[21] Luther is referring here to the abuse of the Lord's Prayer such as took place in connection with prayer beads; cf. Hanns Bächtold-Stäubli, ed., *Handwörterbuch des deutschen Aberglaubens* (Berlin: de Gruyter, 2011), 8:1513–14.

[22] Cf. *Sermon on the Mount* (1530–32/1532), AE 21:60: ". . . light this many little candles to St. Anne."

[23] Translated by Matthew Carver from Martin Luther, *Ungedruckte Predigten D. Martin Luthers aus den Jahren 1537–1540*, ed. Georg Buchwald (Leipzig: G. Strübigs Verlag, 1905), pp. 505–10. Cf. the stenographic notes for this sermon in WA 47:646–52 (Aland Pr 1862).

[24] *Huren und Buben*. The word *Buben* has a range of meaning from "scoundrel" to "philanderer," or, in general, a dissolute, profligate person. By speaking of cohabiting unmarried people as "whores and rakes," Luther is using derogatory language to make such cohabiting shameful.

similar to holy matrimony it is beyond telling, and yet they are whores and rakes and in a sinful condition. Why? God's command is absent. However, if they are married, it is proper, for then it has the proper dress, God's Word. Likewise, thieves and robbers drink and dine together, and it tastes as good to them as it does to those who make a living by manual labor and eat and drink. Indeed, it tastes far better, for there is often house and home, money and goods. Yet in the case of the thieves and robbers, there is only the devil's word. But in the case of those who labor, there is God's Word and command, and you can eat your bread with a good conscience and make use of what you have. In the first case, where it is similar, He says, "I do not want you to have this." Other people's honorable living is completely contrary to yours. A judge sentences someone to hang and be punished on the wheel. Does not the murder and killing committed by the highwayman differ from the hanging and wheel punishment by the judge? Yet there is a great similarity. And nevertheless, the judge has God's command and direction to kill [cf. Rom. 13:4]; the murderer does not. Authorities are to strike, kill, and hang quickly, or else they sin. But if a robber did this and killed, he would be sinning. And so it is not the same work any more than the cohabitation of married people and of whores and rakes are the same. And God says to married people: "You shall live together in holy matrimony," but He forbids whores and rakes to do so. They are not to lie together in unchastity. And this creates the distinction: that holy matrimony is God's institution while God has forbidden fornication.

Thus Baptism is Baptism because it is commanded and ordered by God. Bath attendants and maidservants who wash your feet also have a sort of baptism. Consecrated water, too, is similar. But real Baptism requires, first, that I know that God has commanded it. Therefore, it is a far different cleansing and washing from that which the pope or Turk has, which comes from the imagination of man. But Baptism came from heaven and is a heavenly Baptism and washing of the Holy Spirit. For He commands baptizing. Likewise, He also ordained and instituted it. There is great power in knowing this. For sectarian spirits come along, bringing their own imagination, and saying, "The Church should be governed thus." But as for yourself, say, "No, it should be governed by God's command, and we should be able to say, 'God commanded and ordered this.' " So, too, St. Peter says, "No prophecy was produced by the will of man" [2 Pet. 1:21], but he who teaches, let him teach the Word of God, and if he has something, let him see to it that he does it as God grants him the grace and strength. Only God should be speaking and acting, not you or I. I should be able to say that it was not a man but God who baptized and taught me, for eternal life or eternal damnation depends on this. Absolution should be judged and assessed the same way.

And a judge should also have the assurance that it is not he who sentences or condemns the evildoer to death, but God Himself passes the sentence.

Of course, I am not treating this subject at such length for nothing. Under the papacy I saw firsthand what harm it does when people do not know that it is God commanding or doing something. And the sectarian spirits are eager to make us confess that Baptism is not a divine work and institution. But the salvation of our soul must depend on the true, living, and eternal God, that I may know for certain that He has baptized me and absolved me Himself, and taught me Himself. For this reason Baptism is a heavenly and divine Baptism, even though it is only a handful of water; and the child is baptized not by a man, but by God Himself. Therefore, it is no paltry treasure which is given to us by God's Word. Baptism was instituted not by any man, prophet, or angel, but by God Himself.

The second point relates to the form of the Sacrament—the essence or what the substance of Baptism is. Here say, "It is properly water, but the water has God's Word." The sophists call this the material and the form. Let it be so. Yet for God it is not enough that He gives and orders Baptism; He also prescribed what to say and how to do it, so that, if the first [God's command] should be taken away, our will would not set up a new work or a new mode of baptizing. He said, "Go, baptizing!" [Matt. 28:19]; this is the Word of God. The other part reads: "In the name of the Father, of the Son, and of the Holy Spirit" [Matt. 28:19]; this is the substance or form. Baptism in itself, according to its essence, is water and the words "In the name of the Father and of the Son and of the Holy Spirit." And these two parts are such that they cannot be divided but must be left together. If I say the words and there is no water, it is no Baptism; and, conversely, even if water is present, if the words are not spoken over it, it is no Baptism either. Therefore, Baptism has been so instituted that by definition it consists of water and the words added to it: "In the name of the Father and of the Son and of the Holy Spirit." In other words, I take water and pour it over the child or adult, or dip him in the water, at which point someone says not "I baptize you in my name, as the preacher, or in the name of a nurse," but rather "In the name of God the Father, Son, and Holy Spirit," that is, in the stead of the whole Trinity. Then you know that it is God the Father, the Son, and the Holy Spirit who is baptizing you; I am only supplying my hands for the purpose and speaking the words. Otherwise it is not my Baptism, but God's Baptism. Therefore, you are baptized by God, not baptized by me. It is God's name which is spoken at Baptism. It is very important that we be able to embrace with our heart the fact that in Baptism, the Father, Son, and Holy Spirit is our baptizer. It is He who has the power to make men clean. Therefore, we should not invent new words, but use those which He instituted. Here there is an answer by the sorcerers and practitioners of black magic. They, too, employ these words, make the sign of the holy cross, use the name of the Father, the Son, and the Holy Spirit, and pray five Our Fathers, and even say the Creed, and therefore say, "If the words of God can be used in Baptism, they can certainly be used for our purpose as well, for all the words are sacred."

But two things are required for Baptism: first, the divine command; second, the form of the words. What do the sorceresses and weather charmers lack? They lack God's having commanded it of them. "But they are the same words that are in Baptism!" May the devil thank you! In the papacy there were, and still are today, certain priests who can banish devils, and in order to do so they use very beautiful and holy words, including many good prayers, and the devil acts as if he is afraid of them and seems to flee from them. But he only does so to confirm them in their error. Otherwise he is not afraid. For he thinks: "You may name the Father, Son, and Holy Spirit, but you will not do anything to me, for you have no command to use this against me. Nevertheless, I will depart and flee so that you may be sustained in your error."

Therefore, take care in such matters to see whether the first part—namely, the command of God—is present. If that is absent, it is blasphemy and mockery of God if something is done without His command. All our faith and works are to be so ruled that they keep to His Word and that I may say, "I do this because I know that God has commanded it." Thus I keep my wife in my house because God has given her to me. "What God has joined together, let not man separate" [Matt. 19:6]. Likewise, I eat this bread because God has given it to me. In the same way, all such things in the Christian Church, secular government, and the domestic estate should be done in this faith by which one is assured and certain that it is all so ordained by God. Only Christians know this. All other people know nothing of it. But we Christians have this treasure, and we ought to boast of it and glory in it; for the pope has no such prize and is not very different from a fortune-teller. But we preach it because we know that we have the real Baptism, whether or not we are worthy of it. If I am not worthy to be a pastor, at least I am satisfied that it pleases Him that I am in the pastoral office. One should not say, "I am a husband, but who knows whether that estate pleases God?" No, it must be certain. One must say, "I am baptized. I have partaken of the Sacrament, and have a wife, and it is God's will that it be so." No fornicator can say that.

So also in our passage, there is, first, the command of God against all other purifications and washings, then the form of Baptism: what Baptism is in itself, namely, water combined with God's Word. Here observe that other things do not have these parts. A fornicator has a body just as a husband has, but the command of God is absent. A judge hangs a thief. A highwayman, who provides for himself from his stirrups, also hangs a traveler and takes his money. One deed is like the other. The pope with his consecrated water and sacrifice of the Mass has made a mockery of Baptism and the Sacrament. They are a similar kind of works, yet the pope's is from the devil.

In the same way, then, Baptism is composed of two things: water and the words prescribed by God. And yet to this there is added a third part, namely, the forgiveness of sins. This is the purpose which God has for Baptism, what He seeks and does with it, and what the power and efficacy of Baptism is—not that it takes away the uncleanness of the body nor that it should make a man drunk. No, it does not do that. Rather, its power is that you may become a child of God and may be delivered from the power of the devil, sin, death, and the Law. As the Lord Christ Himself says, "Go, baptizing all nations" [Matt. 28:19]. "Whoever believes and is baptized shall be saved" [Mark 16:16]. Therefore, wherever these three parts of Baptism are found, there is salvation. Baptism brings with it salvation—that is, release from sins—and whoever receives Baptism will, through Baptism, be safe from God and His wrath and judgment, and from sin. Who can express how great a benefit it gives us? So away with all the purifications and ablutions which the pope and the Turks may have! The baptized person is given redemption from sin, from death, and from the judgment and wrath of God. He will be safe and have no doubt that through Baptism he has a gracious God. Dear God, what walking and running about all the monks and nuns have had in order to get a gracious God! Who, having taken up the cowl, has not looked under it to find a gracious God? So also for the same reason they went on pilgrimages to Rome, to Jerusalem, to Santiago. And the pope confirmed that by such things the grace of God could be gained and sins expiated. But if you wish to be a Christian, pull out your Baptism and thrust it in the face of the devil, the pope, and all the sects and say, "I am baptized." If you say this in faith and from your heart, the devil will not remain long. But we cannot say it with such hearts and faith that we are not afraid. We ought to have such courage and confidence in the faith, since God has ordered me to baptize and He Himself has baptized me. For Baptism is God's washing, and I am baptized because He washed me and cleansed me from sins. If you can say that, you have a game that is already won. But if the pope says, "You must make satisfaction for your sins yourself or you will be condemned," do not listen to him, but say, "I am baptized, and I could put a turd in all your holiness. For what are your pilgrimages and ablutions or purifications? I have the washing of the Lord Christ, which has His own blood in it." But they go on: "Still, you have fallen into sin after Baptism." To this let your reply be: "Even if I fall from it, I am nevertheless baptized and am a Christian. I am baptized in God's water, not by some washing maid, not by Gabriel or by the pastor or bishop or pope, but by God the Father, Son, and Holy Spirit. And this washing is consecrated and mingled with the blood of Christ, the Son of God. Why, then, do you come to me with consecrated water, cowls, and tonsures? These things are not the blood of the Son of God. No, I will trust in the washing which He founded and commanded to be administered in the name of the Father and of the Son and of the Holy Spirit and will not regard you, with your consecrated water and washing." God, however, cleanses us not from the uncleanness of the body nor from the uncleanness on our coat, but from sin and death. This He does, moreover, with the water which is mingled with the blood of Christ. This is another washing, ordered by God, having God's Word, and appointed to wash us from sin and death, or to drown the old man.

I could just as easily teach new things too. But I desire to preach, teach, and proclaim what God has ordered to be taught, that it may take root in your hearts to the exclusion of all other washings and acts of worship. For there God's commandment and water and God's Word meet and produce the adoption[25] of God the Father. Learn to understand Baptism this way, contrary to the pope and the craftiness of the devil, who wants all his filth with which he has stained the Christian Church to be regarded as a holy relic. Yet they themselves do not esteem it at all, nor do they believe a thing; and still they are tyrants, compelling and pressing us to go to hell with them. Therefore, we do not know of any[26] forgiveness of sins through pilgrimages, but believe only in the forgiveness of sins through Christ. For there is God's Word. What it says, we shall keep. And He says, "Whoever believes and is baptized shall be saved" [Mark 16:16]. Attached to Baptism, then, is the forgiveness of sins, which comes not through a man or angel but through the Son of God. The holy fathers held Baptism in high esteem. Ambrose calls it a water of blood,[27] and the Supper, blood in the chalice so that the chalice is red. It is as if he would say, "It is a bloody wine." So it is red not from the wine, but from the blood of Christ—this has made it red. In the same way, Baptism is a reddened water. Thus Baptism should not be regarded as the water which cows drink nor by any means be compared to that blasphemous consecrated water! For the pope transfers the effect of Baptism to consecrated water and makes it equal to Baptism, which should not be. Therefore, remember these three points about Baptism.

---

[25] *Kindschaft*, or "the condition of being a child."

[26] Read *Nescimus ullam remissionem* with WA 47:652.11 instead of *Drum wissen wir eine Vergebung* (Buchwald, *Ungedruckte Predigten*, p. 510).

[27] A possible reference to the words "*Unda sanguinis*" in the Ambrosian hymn "Magnae Deus potentiae," stanza 3, line 2.

Third Sermon on Holy Baptism, on the Third Sunday after Epiphany January 26, 1539

I[28] have spoken briefly about the nature of Baptism, that we might know that Baptism is a second and new rebirth by which we are born again to the future, eternal life. I say this in order that we may learn to esteem Baptism highly and know that it is a divine work which was not invented by man. If this understanding of Baptism had remained in the Church under the papacy, various kinds of abomination and idolatry would have been avoided. Whoever believes that, by Baptism, he is made a newborn child of God through the blood of Christ can easily defend himself against those who claim: "Become a monk, and you will be baptized anew!" Let us take this new baptism away from these people! By it they have been wrested away from holy Baptism and think it is no longer worth anything. Truly, God is far greater, and immeasurably greater and more excellent, than the baptism of monkery. Yet Baptism is God's work, not man's work. It is a work established in the blood of the Son of God. It must be incomparably more glorious than monastic life or making pilgrimages, which are only works of man. Yet they hold such human trifles and foolish works greater than the Sacrament of Baptism. What is a pilgrimage? A human trifle. But Baptism is God's work. God is the baptizer. The same goes for the Sacrament of the Altar. Only monasteries and cloisters, not parishes, were regarded as churches. Then people went running to them and giving them money and property, even though there was no Baptism, spoken Word (or preaching office), Absolution, or Supper there. Thus the world fell from God's works to the works of man and only retained a sound, an empty speech, and outward appearance. But set and establish your life on God's Word and work, and whatever else is preached, let it be. However, if there is not Baptism, God's Word, Absolution, etc., do not accept it. You will find this all in your parish far better than getting it in Rome or Jerusalem, for the pope wants to have it in a form other than as God has instituted it. But as high as you hold God above men, so high also hold His work over against the work of man! The pope made laws, and my Baptism was forgotten.

But you have heard that these three things are in Baptism: first, that God's Word, God's institution and consecration, is in it, and that men did not invent it. It is a divine command from heaven which the Lord Christ brought to us. Consecrated water might also be a "baptism," and monks,

---

[28] Translated by Matthew Carver from Martin Luther, *Ungedruckte Predigten D. Martin Luthers aus den Jahren 1537–1540*, ed. Georg Buchwald (Leipzig: G. Strübigs Verlag, 1905), pp. 511–14. Cf. the stenographic notes for this sermon in WA 47:653–59 (Aland Pr 1863).

too, have a "baptism," but it was not ordered or instituted by God, nor did it come from angels, but only from men.

Second, there are also the words here, that is, the form and substance of Baptism, which is that we are to take water and say the words: "I baptize you in the name of the Father and of the Son and of the Holy Spirit." Up to this point sorceresses agree, for they, too, use holy words and names. But that makes it all the worse, for they misuse what is good contrary to God's command, and it would be far better if they said, "I abjure you, cow or calf, in the name of all demons" or "in the name of Lucifer." What is good is not to be used except by God's direction.

Third is the power and strength of Baptism, which is that it grants forgiveness of sins, delivers from death, and makes children of God by the blood and the wounds of the Lord Christ. That is something which sorceresses and petty witches and devil's whores[29] cannot give, nor do they care about the forgiveness of sins or deliverance from death, but only think and consider how one may harm the other. But what God ordains shall be of service to the kingdom of heaven, not to theft.

But before we address the text, let us start with a few admonitions.

The Anabaptists are so clever that they say that children should not be baptized, and those who are baptized in childhood should be rebaptized when they reach the age of reason. The argument goes: children cannot believe because they have no reason or understanding, thus they cannot be given Baptism because they cannot say, "I believe," etc.; accordingly, those who do not believe are not to be given Baptism. Against these fellows you should say that the Lord Christ died not only for the mature but for all mankind [cf. 2 Cor. 5:14]. And when a little child is brought to Baptism, we read the Gospel: "Let the little children come to Me, and do not prevent them, for of such is the kingdom of God" [Mark 10:14]. They bite this verse and chew on it, but they cannot swallow it. They say the term "little children" refers to and means grown, mature people who are humble. However, it is written that the women were bringing little children to Jesus and asking Him to put His hands on them and bless them [Mark 10:13]. They were not carrying old fools to Him. In addition, the Lord Christ says, "Do not prevent them, for of such is the kingdom of God." Therefore, little children should not be prevented from Baptism, for it is not our work.[30] We add nothing to it. It is the work not of a man, but of God. It is God the Father, Son, and Holy Spirit baptizing there. These are the ones really baptizing. Even if it were

[29] *Milchdiebinnen und Teufelshuren*, or "milk thieves and devil's whores," epithets for witches. Regarding these, see above, p. 23 nn. 21–22.

[30] For a fuller explanation of Mark 10:14 and its connection with infant Baptism, see above, pp. 7–9.

possible that children did not have faith (since they cannot give indication of their faith), we should nevertheless believe in a Christian and godly manner that God Himself baptizes the child and gives faith and the Holy Spirit, for this follows from the text. Therefore, let Baptism be regarded as a divine work which God Himself does. A child does not have an evil understanding, nor does he have any heresy. He does not rage and fume against his Baptism.

Second, if the Baptism of children were nothing, little children would not have been really baptized in the Christian Church ever since the apostolic era. Thus if the Baptism of little children were not real, there would have been no Church on earth. Likewise, it would not have given you and me the knowledge of Christ, of His Gospel, and of Baptism. But I know for sure that I have it, and you also, and other Christians who have died in the Christian faith and received the Sacrament and become martyrs and shed their blood. Now then, if their Baptism were not real, God would not have given them the faith and strong courage to give up their lives for it, nor the true understanding and Holy Spirit to be able to preach the faith to others. But God *has* done so.

Therefore, the Anabaptists are foolish and senseless people who like to exalt God and His Church in such a way that the Holy Spirit has nothing to do with it and all Absolution and sacraments must not be real. If they were not real, God would not have sustained and confirmed them and adorned them with such great gifts of the Holy Spirit. Thus Baptism does not distinguish among persons. John says, "I write to old people, to young men and women," etc. [1 John 2:12–14]. Therefore, they are blind, and they fail to take into account that Baptism was commanded or ordered by God, and think it is water such as a cow drinks. But God commanded Baptism; we supply our hands for it, and yet it is His work. For it is not such a thing as when someone normally bathes in water. What must I do if I baptize a scoundrel? I cannot know whether he believes. Here I ask the Anabaptist: "Is Baptism real[31] in that case?" "Indeed," he says. "Why should he not be baptized?" God defend us! Baptism is real even if he who is baptized does not believe. Much more is the Baptism of children real where there is only God's mercy, and in addition such a nature[32] in children as does not oppose God with unbelief. So whether you believe or do not believe, Baptism is real.

Accordingly, we do not grant that children do not believe. They are far better disposed toward Baptism than we are. Baptism is a work established and instituted by God. The preacher adds nothing to it except his hand, just as a carpenter uses the saw and the saw must do the work.

---

[31] *recht*, or "right, valid, legitimate."

[32] *Materie*, or "matter," that upon which God acts.

Thus the Anabaptist says, "If you were baptized in childhood when you were a child, well, then the Baptism is not real, for you did not believe." This does not follow. It is as if you said, "You did not honor your parents, so additional commandments must be made!" Baptism, given once, is genuine and true and abides forever. So even if he who receives it is a scoundrel, no ill is done to Baptism thereby.

To conclude, I would like to talk about emergency Baptism, which is when there is danger and the child cannot be brought to public Baptism. You should not use the false practice of baptizing children before they are born, [arguing that] the soul is in every part of the body, even if there is only a finger.[33] Rather, commend the little child to our Lord God with prayer. But you should not baptize the child unless he has been brought into the world and born. For Baptism is a new birth, as the Lord Christ says in John 3:3. Therefore, Baptism should not be done until he has really and legitimately been born.

Second, if he has been born and is so weak that there is a concern that he cannot survive until he is brought to Baptism, let him be put in the care of the women who know how to treat children. If there is danger, then you women should do the baptizing in each other's company. This Baptism is real only to the extent that it is done with these words: "I baptize you in the name of the Father and of the Son and of the Holy Spirit." It does not matter whether it is done by the midwife or by another honorable matron. Furthermore, let it be done when there is at least a woman or two or three present, or the mother or she whom it most closely concerns. In such emergencies, the women must be "bishopesses"[34] and be able to testify. Do not come to us with that awful business of saying, "I do not know." You must put no doubt in the matter. All truth rests on the mouth of two or three witnesses [Num. 35:30; Deut. 17:6; 19:15; Matt. 18:16; John 8:17; 2 Cor. 13:1; Heb. 10:28]. Anyone who has been baptized once should not be baptized again. In the event that a child is given emergency Baptism and remains alive, bring him before the church and indicate to the pastor that he has been baptized, and let testimony be given at that time. Then the Baptism is [to be] confirmed before the whole world with the imposition of hands. Thus there is to be no rebaptizing, but the Baptism is to be confirmed.

---

[33] This false practice consisted of baptizing a part of the infant before it had been fully born. The stenographic notes for this sermon read here: "Rebirth. 'Unless someone is born again.' Therefore, unless the first birth be completed, the infant is not to be baptized, otherwise it would not be a rebirth. This argument is good against those who assert that the protruding foot of a child in the mother's womb should be baptized, etc." (WA 47:658.38–659.4).

[34] *Bischöfinnen*, i.e., female bishops.

Some people conceal Baptism with silence, and one witness is not to be believed. Baptism must be public, since it is a sacrament of the Church. For this reason, if you wish to deny and rob someone of a Baptism, only be silent.[35] Every Baptism is to be demonstrated. This is why godparents attend, and women are invited, as are the witnesses, who are told: "We ask you to provide your testimony that this little child has been baptized and that his Baptism was confirmed." But if you are alone at the Baptism and do not wish to admit to it, then be silent; but if the child dies in the meantime, let him die, and be a secret baptizer.[36] Therefore, there should always be several women in attendance with women who are giving birth, that they may be able to bear witness. But if they are unable to attend, let the child be baptized. If he dies, however, we will let his Baptism be valid. If you give Baptism in the dark, we cannot pass judgment on the dark. And if an orphaned child is found, and it is unknown whether he has been baptized, go quickly and baptize him, for there is no witness. But if a child is baptized by only one person, so be it! *To us* has been committed a public Baptism, and that is what should be given. *He* may give the secret Baptism!

[35] Apparently this sentence was said in irony.

[36] I.e., do not be concerned about having baptized the child in secret. See also Luther's table talk of fall 1532, recorded by Veit Dietrich, AE 54:56, no. 365; letter to Wenceslas Link, May 12, 1531, AE 50:13–17.

STUDY QUESTIONS

Chapter 1: Infant Baptism and Faith That Is Not One's Own (1525)

Why is it necessary to believe in the true God in order to be saved? (See pp. 3–4.)

Some people think that, according to Rom. 10:17, faith is by definition rational: one must be able to understand words in order to hear God's Word in order to believe that Word and be saved (so they argue). Nowadays, this would lead some people to say that infants should not be baptized. At Luther's time, the Baptism of infants was accepted, but people had different ways of explaining why it was proper. What were these explanations? (See pp. 4–6.)

Does Baptism give faith, or is faith required in advance? (See pp. 4–5, 10–11.)

Infants cannot understand words at an intellectual level, yet Luther argues that the infants we bring to Baptism do in fact believe. What scriptural passages lead him to this conclusion? (See pp. 7–10.)

Why is it important to treat the baptismal ceremony with great reverence? (See p. 11.)

What role do pastors play in Baptism? (See pp. 8–9.)

Chapter 2: Sermons on Holy Baptism (1534)

What does "in the name of" mean in the baptismal formula (Matt. 28:19)? (See pp. 19, 29–31.)

The word "hallowing" means "sanctifying" or "making holy." According to Luther, why is it proper to speak of the water in Baptism as having been hallowed and thus "holy, heavenly," and even "divine"? (See pp. 29, 35.)

Luther illustrates the holiness of Baptism by comparing it to various vocations, such as fatherhood, motherhood, and the office of prince (civil government). What is it that distinguishes each of these from what is common and ordinary? (See pp. 18–19.)

What things must come together for there to be a real Baptism? (See p. 25.)

According to Luther, Baptism must not be based on our faith. Why, then, is faith necessary? (See pp. 20–21, 50, 51–52.)

In what situations can Baptism actually be harmful to someone? (See pp. 28, 57.)

Why was Christ baptized? (See pp. 32–35.)

What does Christ's Baptism reveal about the Baptism that is administered to Christians? (See pp. 35–37.)

Luther likens the words of God the Father at the Baptism of Christ to a baptismal sermon. In what ways are the Father's words similar to our baptismal creed (the Apostles' Creed)? (See p. 37–45.)

The "atonement" is Christ's work to reconcile God to us and us to God. According to God the Father's words at Christ's Baptism, how did Christ make atonement? (See pp. 42–43.)

Baptism provides both initial benefits and ongoing benefits in the lives of Christians. What are some of the initial benefits? How does Luther demonstrate this from Scripture? (See pp. 29–32.)

If Baptism provides salvation (Mark 16:16), what does "salvation" include? (See p. 46.)

What are some of the ongoing benefits of Baptism in the lives of Christians? How does Luther demonstrate this from Scripture? (See pp. 48–49, 54–56.)

In what ways does (or should) Baptism change a person? (See pp. 55–58.)

Chapter 3: Sermons on Holy Baptism (1538)

In the first sermon, Luther speaks of both the preaching of God's Word and the Sacraments as "signs." Why did Christ leave behind these "signs"? (See p. 62.)

Some Christian traditions view "signs" as signifiers or reminders of something absent. For example, if the Lord's Supper is a "sign" of Christ's body and blood, they would see it as a reminder of the absent body and blood of Christ. How does Luther, on the other hand, regard these "signs"? (See p. 66.)

In the first sermon, Luther rebukes people who look for God's will and revelation outside of the Word and Sacraments ("signs"). How does this rebuke challenge you or those in your circles? Why is it important not to seek God outside of His "signs"? (See pp. 64–67.)

In what way are the "signs," especially Baptism, the work of God and not of man? (See pp. 64–65, 67–70, 71–72.)

In what way does the teaching of the ancient Donatists and the sixteenth-century Anabaptists take consolation away from Baptism? (See pp. 70–72.)

In what ways is the creation (Genesis 1) similar to how God works in Baptism? (See p. 72.)

Why does Luther approve of some baptismal ceremonies, such as wearing a white garment, but disapprove of others? (See pp. 75–77.)

Luther emphasizes the ongoing benefits of Baptism by speaking of it as a covenant (a formal, contractual way for two parties to relate to each other—not necessarily a purchase contract). What is the "condition" on the part of the baptized person in order to receive Baptism's benefits? (See pp. 78–79.)

What should happen if a baptized person departs from faith and falls into sin? (See pp. 78–79.)

How should Christians practice fasting? What are its benefits? (See p. 83.)

How is Baptism connected to Christ's merit and atoning death? (See p. 81.)

Much of the fourth sermon is an admonition in which Luther addresses sinful behaviors that were threatening the faith and salvation of his hearers. In what ways does this kind of preaching challenge modern ideas of what preaching should be? (See pp. 84–86.)

How does Luther prove that the Trinity and Christ with His blood is in Baptism? (See pp. 80–82.)

Why did Christ have to be baptized? (See pp. 90–91.)

Compare and contrast the Baptism given by John the Baptist with Christian Baptism. What is the same? What is different? (See pp. 89–93.)

In the Middle Ages, monastic life with its traditions was seen as holy and saving, despite the fact that God had not commanded it. What modern religious practices do people, even Christians, place above Baptism, the Lord's Supper, Absolution, and the preaching of God's Word? (See pp. 86–88.)

Can the covenant of Baptism be broken? How does this teaching provide consolation concerning salvation but, at the same time, avoid security and complacency? (See pp. 93–99.)

How is the kingdom of Christ related to the covenant of Baptism? (See pp. 94–96.)

Why did Christians at Augustine's time (fourth and fifth centuries) think it was good to delay Baptism until a person reached adulthood? How does a proper view of Baptism oppose this attitude? (See pp. 98–99.)

Chapter 4: Sermons on Holy Baptism (1539)

In the first sermon, Luther speaks not of the "means of grace" but more broadly of the means by which the Holy Spirit comes and sanctifies you (makes you holy). He includes the Ten Commandments (the moral Law) as a means by which the Holy Spirit comes and sanctifies. In what way does the Law function as a means by which the Holy Spirit sanctifies people? (See pp. 102–6.)

Luther speaks of three categories of actions performed in the context of the Christian Church: those that are commanded by God, those that are permitted by God if not misused, and those that are being used for wrongful purposes. Give examples of each. How should the ancient Christian customs be regarded? (See pp. 103–6.)

What is it that distinguishes Baptism from other religious washings and makes Baptism holy and sanctifying? (See pp. 102, 105–6.)

Why does Luther continuously emphasize the importance of God's commands (recorded in Scripture)? (See pp. 108–10.)

In Baptism, what do the words "In the name of the Father, and of the Son, and of the Holy Spirit" mean? (See pp. 108–10.)

What are some false ways in which people strive to be rid of their sins and the evil in their lives, both at Luther's time and now? (See pp. 102–4, 111–12.)

In the third sermon, Luther says that even if infants did not believe, God would give faith as a benefit of Baptism. Yet he argues that infants in the context of the Church do believe. If they already believe before Baptism, what benefits are left for Baptism to give? (See pp. 114–15.)

At the end of the third sermon, Luther deals with emergency Baptism and the public character of Baptism. Baptism must have two or three witnesses. In emergencies where it is impossible to have witnesses, Baptism should still be given. Elsewhere Luther explains that an infant baptized by its mother with no witnesses should be baptized again in church (if the infant survives), since there were no witnesses. Why did Luther consider two or three witnesses so necessary? (See pp. 116–17.)

ABBREVIATIONS

AE	*Luther's Works: American Edition*. Volumes 1–30: Edited by Jaroslav Pelikan. St. Louis: Concordia, 1955–76. Volumes 31–55: Edited by Helmut Lehmann. Philadelphia/Minneapolis: Muhlenberg/Fortress, 1957–86. Volumes 56–82: Edited by Christopher Boyd Brown and Benjamin T. G. Mayes. St. Louis: Concordia: 2009–.
Aland	Kurt Aland. *Hilfsbuch zum Lutherstudium*. Fourth edition. Bielefeld: Luther-Verlag, 1996. Cited by main catalog number, postil number (Po), sermon number (Pr), or letter number (Br).
ARG	*Archiv für Reformationsgeschichte*
Brecht	Martin Brecht. *Martin Luther*. Translated by James L. Schaaf. 3 volumes. Minneapolis: Fortress, 1985–93.
Concordia	*Concordia: The Lutheran Confessions*. Second edition. St. Louis: Concordia, 2006.
DWB	Jacob Grimm and Wilhelm Grimm. *Deutsches Wörterbuch*. 16 volumes in 32. Leipzig: S. Hirzel, 1854–1960.
E^2	*Dr. Martin Luther's sämmtliche Werke*. Second edition. 26 volumes in 27. Frankfurt and Erlangen: Heyder & Zimmer, 1862–85.
FC	*Fathers of the Church*. Edited by Ludwig Schopp. New York: Fathers of the Church, 1947–.
Kolb-Wengert	Robert Kolb and Timothy J. Wengert, eds. *The Book of Concord: The Confessions of the Evangelical Lutheran Church*. Minneapolis: Fortress, 2000.
Lenker	John Nicholas Lenker, ed. *Sermons of Martin Luther: The Church Postils*. Grand Rapids: Baker Books, 1996 (8 volumes in 4; reprinted as volumes 1–4 of *The Complete Sermons of Martin Luther.* Grand Rapids: Baker Books, 2000. Originally published as volumes 7–14 of *The Precious and Sacred Writings of Martin Luther*. Minneapolis: Lutherans in All Lands/Luther Press, 1904–9).
LTK^2	Josef Höfer and Karl Rahner, eds. *Lexikon für Theologie und Kirche*. Second edition. 14 volumes. Freiburg im Breisgau: Herder, 1957–68.
LTK^3	Walter Kasper et al., eds. *Lexikon für Theologie und Kirche*. Third edition. 11 volumes. Freiburg im Breisgau: Herder, 1993–2001.

NPNF[1] *A Select Library of the Christian Church: Nicene and Post-Nicene Fathers: First Series.* Edited by Philip Schaff. 14 volumes. New York, 1886–89. Reprint, Peabody, MA: Hendrickson, 1994.

NPNF[2] *A Select Library of the Christian Church: Nicene and Post-Nicene Fathers: Second Series.* Edited by Philip Schaff and Henry Wace. 14 volumes. New York, 1890–1900. Reprint, Peabody, MA: Hendrickson, 1994.

ODCC F. L. Cross, ed. *The Oxford Dictionary of the Christian Church.* Third edition revised. Oxford: Oxford University Press, 2005.

OER *The Oxford Encyclopedia of the Reformation.* Edited by Hans J. Hillerbrand. New York: Oxford University Press, 1996.

PL *Patrologiae cursus completus: Series Latina.* Edited by J.-P. Migne. 221 volumes in 223. Paris: Garnier Fratres, 1844–64.

ST Thomas Aquinas. *Summa theologiae.* Edited by Thomas Gilby et al. 61 volumes. Oxford: Blackfriars, 1964–. Reprint, Cambridge: Cambridge University Press, 2006. Also Fathers of the English Dominican Province, trans. *Summa Theologica.* 3 volumes. New York: Benziger, 1947–48.

TRE *Theologische Realenzyklopädie.* Edited by Gerhard Krause and Gerhard Müller. Berlin: de Gruyter, 1977–.

WA *D. Martin Luthers Werke: Kritische Gesamtausgabe.* 73 volumes in 85. Weimar: H. Böhlau, 1883–.

WA Br *D. Martin Luthers Werke: Briefwechsel.* 18 volumes. Weimar: H. Böhlau, 1930–.

WA DB *D. Martin Luthers Werke: Deutsche Bibel.* 12 volumes in 15. Weimar: H. Böhlau, 1906–.

Wander Karl Friedrich Wilhelm Wander. *Deutsches Sprichwörter-Lexikon.* Leipzig: Brockhaus, 1867–80. Reprint, Darmstadt: Wissenschaftliche Buchgesellschaft, 2007. Cited by volume and page, then word and number, e.g., Wander 2:212, "Gott" no. 22.

INDEX OF PERSONS AND GROUPS

Agatha (saint, d. ca. 251), 23
Ambrose of Milan (ca. 339–397), 83, 88, 112
Anne (saint), 107
Anthony of Egypt (ca. 251–356), 87
Augustine (354–430), 4, 5, 20, 21, 23, 69, 71, 74, 76, 83, 86, 87n, 98
Aurifaber, Johann (1519–75), xixn, xx, xxi–xxiv

Beguines, 87
Benedict of Nursia (ca. 480–ca. 547), 86, 102
Bernard of Clairvaux (1090–1153), 86, 87
Blaise (saint, d. 316), 23
Brown, Christopher Boyd, xiii, xx
Buchwald, Georg (1859–1947), xxii

Carthusians, 90, 92, 94, 96, 103, 105
Carver, Matthew, xiii, xx, xxi
Catabaptists, 68
Constantine (emperor, r. 306–337), 98
Cyprian (bishop of Carthage, ca. 210–258), 21, 50, 52

Dietrich of Bern. *See* Theodoric the Great
Dominicans, 74, 94
Donatists, 68–69

Enthusiasts, 19–20n
Epicureans, 13

Francis of Assisi (ca. 1181–1226), 86, 92, 102
Franciscans, 94

Gregory I (pope, r. 590–604), 83, 87
Grudem, Wayne, ix

Jerome (ca. 345–420), xi, 77, 94, 98, 104
John Frederick (elector, r. 1532–47), 83

Langebartels, James L., xiii
Lauterbach, Anton (1502–69), xix
Leo X (pope, r. 1513–21), 5
Luther, Martin (1483–1546), Baptism doctrine of, x–xii, xvii–xxi; baptismal preaching of, xii–xiii, xvi–xxi; baptismal writings of, xv–xvi; correspondence of, xxi–xxii; justification doctrine of, x; sermons of, xv, xvi, xxii; table talk of, xxii
Luther, Martin (writings of): *Babylonian Captivity of the Church* (1520), xv, xvii, 72n; *Concerning Rebaptism* (1528), xv, xvii, 7n; *Concerning the Order of Public Worship* (1523), xviin; *Holy and Blessed Sacrament of Baptism* (1519), xv; *Infant Baptism and Faith That Is Not One's Own* (1525), xv, 3–12; *Large Catechism* (1529), xn, xin, xiin, xv, xviiin, xix; *Lent Postil* (1525), xv, xvii; *Order of Baptism* (1523), 90n; *Order of Baptism Newly Revised* (1526), 90n; *Sermons at the Baptism of Bernhard of Anhalt* (1540), xvi; *Sermons on Holy Baptism*

(1534), xx, 13–59; *Sermons on Holy Baptism* (1538), xx–xxi, 61–99; *Sermons on Holy Baptism* (1539), xxi, 101–17; *Sermons on Matthew 18–24* (1537–40), xixn; *Smalcald Articles* (1537), 67, 106, *Small Catechism* (1529), xv, xix, 25; *Ten Sermons on the Catechism* (1528), xv

Manichaeans, 98

Martin of Tours (bishop, ca. 336–397), 66

Poach, Andreas (1515–85), xxi

Ramsey, Patrick, x

Rörer, Georg (1492–1557), xix, xx, xxi, xxii–xiv

Scotus, John Duns (ca. 1265–1308), 74

Servetus, Michael (1511–53), 13–14n

Stolz, Johann (ca. 1514–56), xx

Theodoric the Great (454–526), 38n

Thomas Aquinas (ca. 1225–74), 74

Waldensians (Bohemian Brethren, Unity of Brethren), 5–7

Zwingli, Ulrich (1484–1531), xv

SCRIPTURE INDEX

Old Testament

Genesis

1:14–18 27
1:20 .... 72, 74
1:28 .... 62, 72
3:15 62

Exodus

19:16 44
19:18 44
20:3 85
20:7 .... 30, 31

Leviticus

15 21

Numbers

16:32 56
19:22 21
35:30 116

Deuteronomy

6:4 40
17:6 116
19:15 116

2 Samuel

7:14 39

1 Chronicles

22:10 39

Job

38:7 39

Psalms

2:7 89
32:9 17
60:4 65
67:36 9
68:35 9
82:6 .... 40n
89:27 39
110:4 42
116:11 54
117:2 55
146:3 54

Isaiah

2:22 54
4:6 95
53:5 80
55:9 9

Jeremiah

17:5 54

Hosea

11:1 9

Apocrypha

Ecclesiasticus (Sirach)

34:4 .... 21, 52, 68

New Testament

Matthew

2:2 14
3 .... 86n, 89
3:1–17 86
3:2 89
3:4 89
3:7 90
3:11 .... 33, 90
3:11–12 89
3:13–17 .... ix, xix, 14, 32, 102
3:14 91
3:15 .... x, 91
3:16 .... 77, 91
3:16–17 93,
3:17 .... xxi, 37, 88, 92
6:12 51
7:21 91
8:1–13 .... 3n
16:19 .... 88, 96
17:5 .... 77, 95, 97
18:3 9
18:16 116
18:18 .... 88, 96
19:6 110
19:13–15 8
19:14 .... 81, 112
23:35 63
23:37 97
24:15 64
24:26 65
25:1–13 76
26:26–27 25
28:19 .... ix, 22, 35, 36, 71, 73, 74, 106, 109, 111

Mark

1:9–11 ix
10:13 114
10:13–16 8
10:14 .... 12, 114
16:15 71
16:15–16 88
16:16 .... xx, 3, 5, 8, 21, 22, 27, 31, 46, 50, 77, 78, 111, 112

Luke

1:44 xviii
2:11 91
2:42–52 .... 61n
3:21–22 ix
11:26 59
18:15 8
18:15–16 8
18:16 8
22:19 .... 26, 75
22:19–20 26

John

1:1–14 .... 101n, 107n
1:13 87
1:14 105
1:32–34 ix
2:1–12 .... 61n
2:11 14
3:1–5 ix
3:3 116
3:5 .... 4, 73
3:6 80
3:16 .... 3, 36
3:18 3
8:12 98
8:17 116
8:44 .... 26, 85
13:33 9
14:6 98
20:23 .... 88, 96

Romans

1:17 3
3:4 27
6:4 .... ix, 56
10:17 .... 4, 9
13:4 108

1 Corinthians

1:12 76
1:13–14 76
6:11 ix
10:2 54
11:24–25 75
11:29 58
12:13 ix

2 Corinthians

5:14 114
11:14 105
13:1 116

Galatians

1:8 .... 87, 89, 92, 102
3:26–28 ix

Ephesians

1:22 86
4:5 7
4:15 86
5:26 .... ix, 73

Colossians

2:8 86
2:11 ix
2:20 ix
3:1 ix
3:3–4 ix

1 Timothy

1:9 .... xin

2 Timothy

4:3–4 86

Titus

2:10 59
2:13 82
3:3–8 ix
3:5 .... 27, 31, 73, 75, 82

Hebrews

1:5 39
4:14 98
7:25 42
10:23 ix
10:28 116

1 Peter

2:24 56
2:25 96
3:21 .... ix, 7
5:4 95
5:8 85

2 Peter

1:17–21 92
1:21 .... 88, 108
2:20 59
2:20–22 48

1 John

2:1 97
2:12–14 115
2:13 9
5:7–8 73

Jude

4 59

Revelation

13:8 78